The Law of Cooperatives

Charles T. Autry
Roland F. Hall

AMERICAN BAR ASSOCIATION
Business Law Section

Commitment to Quality: The ABA Section of Business Law is committed to quality in our publications. Our authors are experienced practitioners in their fields. Prior to publication, the contents of our books are rigorously reviewed by experts to ensure the highest quality product and presentation. Because we are committed to serving our readers' needs, we welcome your feedback on how we can improve future editions of this book.

Original cover design by Tamara Nowak.

The materials contained herein represent the opinions of the authors and editors and should not be construed to be the action of either the American Bar Association or the Section of Business Law unless adopted pursuant to the bylaws of the Association.

Nothing contained in this book is to be considered as the rendering of legal advice for specific cases, and readers are responsible for obtaining such advice from their own legal counsel. This book and any forms and agreements herein are intended for educational and informational purposes only.

No part of the publication may be reproduced, stored in a retrieval system, or transmitted in any form or by any means, electronic, mechanical, photocopying, recording, or otherwise, without the prior written permission of the publisher. Permission requests should be sent to the American Bar Association Copyrights & Contracts Department via e-mail at copyright@abanet.org or via fax at (312) 988-6030.

© 2009 by the American Bar Association. All rights reserved. Printed in the United States of America.

09 08 07 06 05 5 4 3 2 1

Library of Congress Cataloging-in-Publication Data

Hall, Roland F., 1969–
  The law of cooperatives / Roland Hall, Charles T. Autry.
    p. cm.
  Includes index.
  ISBN 978-1-60442-309-9 (alk. paper)
 1. Cooperative societies—Law and legislation—United States. 2. Cooperative societies—United States. I. Autry, Charles T. II. Title.

  KF1470.H35 2009
  346.73'0668—dc22

2009012490

Discounts are available for books ordered in bulk. Special consideration is given to state and local bars, CLE programs, and other bar-related organizations. Inquire at Book Publishing, American Bar Association, 321 North Clark Street, Chicago, Illinois 60654-7598.

For a complete list of ABA publications, visit www.ababooks.org.

For Donna, Michael, Kelly, and Catherine
C.T.A.

For Anna, Hannah, Lillian, and Amelia
R.F.H.

Preface and Acknowledgments

As attorneys who regularly perform work for cooperatives, we have found that there are excellent resources that address specific issues of cooperative law, such as cooperative taxation. We have found far fewer resources for the practitioner who is unfamiliar with cooperatives and seeks a general guide to cooperative law. Most publications and articles addressing issues related to cooperatives presume that the reader is already familiar with the cooperative structure and vocabulary. This book is intended to provide the practitioner with an overview of the primary issues that differentiate cooperative law from other areas of business law.

The information in this book comes from our combined experience in working for cooperatives, as well as from our research into aspects of cooperative law with which we were less familiar. In the process of attempting to educate others about cooperatives, we found that we were educating ourselves as well.

This book is intended to be an introduction to cooperative law, rather than an exhaustive treatment of the subject. Accordingly, we have used endnotes where doing so would be helpful in providing the reader with additional resources concerning a specific issue. In some chapters we have also listed further reading that give additional information on selected topics.

A number of individuals assisted us with this book and deserve our recognition. We thank David Cook, our associate, for his invaluable assistance with all issues related to cooperative taxation. We also thank Jessica A. Rissmiller, our research assistant, now practicing in Atlanta, Georgia, for her able assistance. Special thanks and appreciation are owed to Professor Harold S. Lewis of the Mercer University School of Law, and to Professor Thomas E. Geu of the University of South Dakota School of Law, who provided extremely helpful advice and editorial suggestions. Finally, we thank the Editorial Board and staff of the Business Law Section of the American Bar Association for their assistance in bringing this book to fruition. Of course, we alone are responsible for any errors or omissions.

Contents

Preface and Acknowledgments   v

I   Introduction to the Cooperative Entity   1

A. Basic Description of Cooperative Form of Business   1
B. Importance of Cooperatives in the United States and World Economies   3

Notes   5

II   History and Attributes of the Cooperative Form of Business   7

A. Defining the Cooperative   7
B. Cooperative Principles   8
C. Origin of the Cooperative Form of Business   10
  1. Emergence of the Modern Cooperative   10
  2. Early American Cooperatives   12
  3. Development of Cooperatives After the Civil War   13
  4. New Types of Cooperatives   19

Notes   22
Further Reading   24

III   Using the Cooperative Form of Business   25

A. Comparison of the Cooperative Entity With Other Business Entities   26
  1. Return on Investment and Financing Techniques   27

vii

viii   **Contents**

      2. Business Purpose, Ownership and Control, and Distribution of Income   29
      3. Taxation   31
  B. When to Use the Cooperative Form   32
      1. Restrictions on Lines of Business   34
      2. Restrictions on Outside Investment and Payment of Dividends   35
      3. Control and the Decision-Making Process   35
      4. Conclusion   36
  C. Formation of Cooperatives   36

IV   Types of Cooperatives and Cooperative Structure   41

  A. Classification by Business Purpose   42
      1. Restrictions on Lines of Business   42
      2. Categories of Cooperatives by Business Purpose   44
  B. Classification by Structure   49
      1. Centralized Cooperatives   50
      2. Federated Cooperatives   51
      3. Hybrid or Mixed Cooperatives   51
Notes   52
Further Reading   52

V   Operation and Governance   53

  A. Members   53
      1. Members and Their Relationship with the Cooperative   54
      2. Governance Powers of Members   55
  B. Directors   56
      1. Selection and Compensation   57
      2. Distinctive Characteristics of the Cooperative Board   58
      3. Liability and Training   59
  C. Officers and Management   60
  D. The Duties of Officers and Directors   62
      1. Duty of Care   62
      2. Duty of Loyalty   63
      3. Duty of Obedience   65
      4. Minimizing Liability   65
      5. Liability, Indemnity and Insurance   67

E. Contractual Relationships Between the Cooperative and
    Its Members   68
Notes   69
Further Reading   70

VI   Capitalization and Finance   71

A. Comparison of Stock Cooperatives and Nonstock
   Cooperatives   71
   1. Stock Cooperatives   72
   2. Nonstock Cooperatives   74
B. Capital   74
   1. Equity Capital   75
   2. Debt Capital   77
C. Net Margins and Patronage Refunds   79
D. Equity Redemption Plans   82
Notes   85
Further Reading   86

VII   Taxation of Cooperatives   87

A. What Is a Cooperative for Federal Tax Purposes?   87
B. Is the Cooperative a Taxable Entity?   88
C. If the Cooperative Is a Taxable Entity, How Is the Cooperative
   Taxed?   90
D. Regular Corporate Taxation With Special Benefits to
   Cooperatives   90
   1. Subchapter T Cooperatives   91
      a. *Applicability of Subchapter T*   91
      b. *Special Deductions*   91
      c. *Definitions Applicable to Subchapter T*   92
         i. Patronage Earnings and Losses   92
         ii. Patronage Dividends   92
         iii. Written Notice of Allocation (Qualified and
              Nonqualified)   94
         iv. Per-Unit Retain Allocation and Certificate   95
      d. *Types of Special Deductions*   95
         i. Special Deductions for Patronage Dividends Paid
            as Money, Property, or Qualified Written Notices
            of Allocation   95

- ii. Special Deductions for Redemption of Nonqualified Written Notices of Allocation   96
- iii. Special Deductions for Per-Unit Retain Allocations   96
- iv. Special Deductions for Redemption of Nonqualified Per-Unit Retain Certificates   96
- v. Special Deductions for Section 521 Farmers' Cooperatives—Dividends on Capital Stock   97
- vi. Special Deductions for Section 521 Farmers' Cooperatives—Distributions from Non-Patronage Earnings and U.S. Government Sources   97
- vii. Special Deductions for Section 521 Farmers' Cooperatives—Redemptions Related to Non-Patronage Sources and U.S. Government Sources   98
- e. *Timing Rules for Special Deductions*   98
- f. *Special Tax Computation of Subchapter T Cooperatives*   99
- g. *Taxation of Subchapter T Patrons*   101
2. Section 521 Farmers' Cooperatives   102
    - a. *Applicability of Section 521*   102
    - b. *Effect of Subchapter T on Section 521 Farmers' Cooperatives*   103
    - c. *Flexibility of Section 521 Farmers' Cooperatives*   103
    - d. *Nondiscrimination Rules*   103
3. Other Cooperative Organizations   104
    - a. *Cooperative Housing Corporations*   104
    - b. *Cooperative Banks*   105

E. Tax Exemption   106

1. Section 501(c)(12) Cooperatives   106
    - a. *Applicability of § 501(c)(12)*   106
        - i. Eligible Organizations and Purposes   106
        - ii. Operation on a Cooperative Basis   107
        - iii. The Member Income Test   108
    - b. *Unrelated Business Income Tax*   108
2. Section 501(c)(14)—Credit Unions   108
3. Section 501(c)(16)—Cooperative Organizations to Finance Section 521 Farmers' Cooperative's Crop Operations   109
4. Section 501(e)—Cooperative Hospital Service Organizations   109

5. Section 501(f)—Cooperative Service Organization of an
   Operating Educational Organization   110
F. Conclusion   110
Notes   110

Table of Cases   121
Index   123
About the Author   127

Introduction to the Cooperative Entity

Most business law courses in universities and law schools touch lightly, if at all, on the cooperative business form. Students learn about the intricacies of corporations, partnerships, limited liability companies, and other more exotic business forms, but they are rarely exposed to the cooperative form, even though a substantial number of business transactions are conducted by or with businesses organized as cooperatives. This book is designed to fill the gap and provide an introduction to the cooperative entity and to the law of cooperatives.

Why is it important to know about the cooperative form of business? In our experience, attorneys who have had limited exposure to the cooperative form often face a steep learning curve when negotiating with cooperatives on behalf of their clients or when attempting to represent a new client that happens to be organized as a cooperative. Although cooperatives are similar in many respects to other businesses, certain characteristics are distinctly different and not necessarily intuitive to an attorney familiar with corporations and partnerships. Also, clients seeking to form a new business might be well advised to use the cooperative form under certain circumstances, but such advice must be based on at least a working knowledge of the cooperative form and its advantages and disadvantages vis-à-vis other types of business entities.

A. Basic Description of Cooperative Form of Business

Assuming, then, that knowledge of the cooperative form is useful, what is a cooperative? Although economic and "legal" definitions of the cooperative entity will be provided later in this book, a cooperative business generally

1

has the following characteristics: (1) It is owned and controlled by the people who use its services or buy its products (its "owner/customers"); (2) its primary focus is to provide its services or goods to its owner/customers and not to the general public; (3) it is democratically controlled by its owner/customers, and each owner/customer has one vote regardless of the amount of services or products it purchases from the cooperative; and (4) the primary objective of the cooperative is to maximize benefits to its owner/customers rather than profits.

The development of the cooperative form is unique in comparison to that of other business entities in that the modern cooperative form was largely developed by individuals and small businesses reacting to the emergence of large business entities, such as corporations and limited partnerships, and seeking a way to successfully compete with these larger businesses, in both selling their goods and purchasing needed services or supplies. Smaller buyers and producers found that they could leverage their buying and selling power by joining together in groups. While a single individual or small business might find itself at the mercy of the prices and policies of a large business, representatives of a group of such cooperating buyers or producers could obtain more favorable prices and terms. The cooperative form was also developed as a way to provide services or goods that would otherwise be unavailable, either because the cooperative's members lacked the capital or expertise to provide such services or goods by themselves or because the particular market was too small to interest larger businesses. It was the need to establish an economic and legal framework for such cooperative entities that led, over the course of many years, and through many failed experiments, to the generally accepted principles and characteristics that make up the modern cooperative.

Cooperatives are also unique in comparison to other business entities because of the differing treatment that they receive from the federal and state governments in comparison to the treatment given other business entities. The basis for such differing treatment arises from policies tied to the basic nature of cooperatives. The rewards from their operations go almost entirely to their owner/customers rather than to outside investors, and in many cases, they provide services or products that would otherwise be unavailable from investor-owned enterprises. Preferences were given to cooperatives in the early twentieth century in response to the success of agricultural cooperatives in helping individual farmers rise from economic depression. The success of such preferences then led to policy makers using the preferences to create opportunities for cooperatives, as in the case of rural electric and telephone cooperatives, which were able to provide services to rural Americans not available from larger entities, in part because of tax advantages and opportunities for low-cost, government-backed financing. While preferences continue to be extended to some cooperatives today, in some cases, governments have also imposed restrictions on cooperatives based on their unique characteristics.

In addition to the practical and legal differences discussed, there are also important intangible differences between the cooperative and other business entities. For example, the attorney representing or negotiating with a cooperative will often find a distinctive pride of ownership among a cooperative's owner/customers. Although consumers have brand loyalty to corporations, only with the cooperative does the owner/customer have the ability to directly govern the course of the business and control the quality of the product or service. Owner/customers of cooperatives, if asked about the benefits of their cooperative, will often focus not only on the price of goods and services or the quality of management, but also on their ability to control the quality of goods and services, to interact with other owner/customers, and to directly control the direction of the business.

Another characteristic of the cooperative is not so much a required element as it is an unavoidable by-product of the cooperative form and the reasons for its development. Because cooperatives are formed by their owners for the specific purpose of providing a particular service or product, for the most part the cooperative is primarily focused on the delivery of one product or service. While the typical business concern is willing to enter into any line of business, provided it produces a profit for its partners or shareholders, the cooperative tends not to stray far from the original purpose for which it was founded. Also, unlike other business entities, cooperatives are required in many cases to limit their activities by statute or because of the specter of unfavorable tax consequences.

All of these characteristics of the cooperative entity have acted in combination to make cooperatives, regardless of their size, the "stealth businesses" of our economy. Because cooperatives operate primarily for the benefit of their owner/customers, and not for the general public, cooperatives typically advertise less than other businesses do and have less need to establish public "brands." Also, because cooperatives are not owned by outside investors and they typically have no SEC (U.S. Securities and Exchange Commission) reporting requirements, public data on the financial activities of cooperatives usually is not publicly available, and the media and financial community have no reason to place cooperatives in the limelight. For these and other reasons, although cooperatives provide a wide variety of products and services to a substantial number of consumers and have a sizeable impact on our economy, most people are unfamiliar not only with the role of cooperatives in the economy, but also with the characteristics of the cooperative entity itself. Before examining these characteristics in detail, it is worth taking a side trip to briefly explore the actual impact of cooperatives on the economies of the United States and of countries throughout the world.

B. Importance of Cooperatives in the United States and World Economies

The economic importance of cooperatives makes a compelling case for obtaining a working knowledge of the cooperative entity. There are over 47,000 cooperatives in operation in the United States today, with those cooperatives serving almost 120 million members.[1] Statistics show that, in 2007, just the top 100 revenue-producing cooperatives in the United States had over $170 billion in revenues.[2] Clearly cooperatives play an important role in the U.S. economy.

How is it that cooperatives have such a widespread impact on the economy? While most people are aware of certain types of cooperatives, such as agricultural or electric cooperatives, cooperatives actually produce or deliver a wide variety of goods and services, including health care, insurance, telecommunications, financial services, child care, housing, and consumer products such as hardware and groceries. These types of cooperatives are often referred to as consumer cooperatives. Other types of cooperatives have a strong economic impact as well. For example, marketing cooperatives, which include agricultural cooperatives, sell the products of their members into the relevant market.

Many well-known businesses with established brand names are cooperatives, even though consumers might not be aware of them as such. Familiar names include Ace Hardware, a retailers cooperative with over three billion dollars in revenues whose owner/members operate over 4600 independent stores; Land O'Lakes, a national agricultural marketing cooperative that is one of the largest producers of butter and cheese in the country and which directly employs over 6000 workers; Sunkist Growers, a citrus growers cooperative with over 6000 members that has licensed its brand name for use on over 600 products; and the Associated Press, a news agency owned by its 1500 daily newspaper members.

Cooperatives in certain other industries are not recognized as such, although their brands are well known. For example, the mutual insurance company, in which policyholders have certain ownership rights in the company, is a form of cooperative, with larger mutual insurers including Nationwide Mutual Insurance Company, Mutual of Omaha, and State Farm Insurance. Credit unions are also cooperative entities and, as a group in the United States, have over 85 million members and assets of over $700 billion.[3] Also, while cooperatives in some other industries are certainly recognized as cooperative entities, their impact and scope are less recognized. For example, over 860 distribution electric cooperatives (cooperatives that provide power directly to consumers) serve more than 40 million people in 47 states.[4] More than 1.2 million families live in homes owned by cooperative housing associations located across the country.[5]

Cooperatives play an important role not only in the United States, but around the world. The International Co-operative Alliance, an organization formed in 1895 to represent and serve cooperatives worldwide, first began to collect statistics on cooperatives in 1897 and recently estimated that over 800 million people worldwide are members of cooperatives.[6] Its collected statistics indicate that cooperatives provide over 100 million jobs worldwide, and that cooperatives unquestionably have a significant positive impact on national economies throughout the world.[7]

The worldwide significance and impact of the cooperative entity has not gone unnoticed. The United Nations declared 1995 to be the "International Year of Cooperation." During his term as Secretary-General of the United Nations, Kofi Annan said that cooperatives "provide vital health, housing and banking services; they promote education and gender equality; they protect the environment and workers' rights. Through these and a range of other activities, they help people in more than a hundred countries better their lives and those in their communities."[8] The United Nations has recognized that cooperatives can play a special role in increasing economic and social progress in both developed and developing countries, and in 2005, a report of the Secretary-General stated that "[u]nlike other types of private sector business organizations, cooperatives subscribe to a set of core values and principles . . . which emphasize social responsibility and community development."[9] The increasing international recognition of cooperatives was further enhanced in 2000, when the Internet Corporation for Assigned Names and Numbers (ICANN), the international body responsible for global coordination of the use of Internet domain names and addresses, approved use of the .coop extension for use by cooperatives.

Having discussed the distinctive nature of the cooperative entity and its importance in our economy and in economies worldwide, let us now turn to a fuller description of the cooperative entity and a brief history of its development. The brief history presented in the next chapter is not intended to be exhaustive, but we hope it will provide additional context within which to understand the cooperative's emergence, rapid expansion, and still-evolving characteristics.

Notes

1. National Cooperative Bank, *NCB Co-op 100*, *available at* http://www.ncb.coop.

2. *Id.*

3. National Credit Union Association, *Credit Unions Post Solid Asset Growth in 2006* (February 21, 2007), *available at* http://www.ncua.gov/news/press_releases/2007/MR07-0221.htm.

4. National Rural Electric Cooperative Association, *Co-ops by the Numbers*, *available at* http://www.nreca.org/AboutUs/Co-op101/CooperativeFacts.htm.

5. National Association of Housing Cooperatives, *About NAHC & Housing Co-ops, available at* http://www.coophousing.org/about_nahc.shtml.

6. International Co-operative Alliance, *Statistical Information on the Co-operative Movement, available at* http://www.ica.coop/members/member-stats.html.

7. *Id.*

8. United Nations, *Cooperatives at Work, available at* http://www.un.org/issues/calendar/cache/Cooperatives.pdf.

9. The Secretary-General, *Report of the Secretary-General on Cooperatives in Social Development,* ¶ 8, *delivered to the General Assembly,* U.N. DOC. A/60/138 (July 21, 2005).

History and Attributes of the Cooperative Form of Business

Because the legal framework for cooperatives was only recently established in the United States, and in fact remains in transition today, it is helpful to examine the attributes of the cooperative and the history of its development to fully understand what a cooperative is and why cooperatives are formed. We will first examine the definition of the cooperative and the principles of cooperative operation and will then turn to a brief history of the development of the cooperative entity. Finally, we will take a look at new forms of the cooperative being developed today.

A. Defining the Cooperative

Attempting to define a *cooperative* is difficult precisely because the cooperative model can be adapted to so many different types of business enterprises. Over seventy years ago, Justice Brandeis of the U.S. Supreme Court noted in a dissenting opinion that "no one plan of organization is to be labeled as truly co-operative to the exclusion of others."[1] More recently, it has been said that there is "no universally accepted definition of a cooperative."[2] To understand when the modern form of cooperative was first developed, however, it is necessary to know what a cooperative is considered today. The first requirement is thus to establish a working definition that captures the characteristics of the modern cooperative entity.

One commonly used definition of the cooperative was developed by the International Co-operative Alliance (ICA), the organization that represents cooperatives worldwide. The ICA defines a cooperative as a voluntary association of persons united to meet their common economic, social, and cultural needs through a jointly owned and democratically controlled enterprise. It is obvious from this definition that the ICA intends cooperatives to do more than serve the economic interests of their members. The ICA in fact states that cooperation

> at its best aims at something beyond promotion of the individual members who compose a cooperative at any time. Its object is rather to promote the progress and welfare of humanity. It is this aim that makes a co-operative society something different from an ordinary economic enterprise and justifies its being tested, not simply from the stand point of its business efficiency, but also from the standpoint of its contribution to the moral and social values which elevate human life above the merely material and animal.[3]

As can be seen from this statement, in other societies, particularly in developing countries, cooperatives are seen as an agent for moral and social change as well as economic change.

Although the ICA's definition captures the spirit of the cooperative organization, for our purposes in this book, a more focused working definition is necessary that cleanly distinguishes cooperatives from other business forms commonly used in the United States. The U.S. Department of Agriculture (USDA) has provided such a definition that is widely accepted in the United States: A cooperative is a user-owned, user-controlled business that distributes benefits on the basis of use.[4] This means that

- those who use the cooperative's goods and services own the cooperative;
- those who use and own the cooperative have democratic control over the cooperative, typically through a one-member/one-vote policy; and
- benefits from the cooperative are returned to its owner/users on the basis of their use of the cooperative during the year.

While other types of business entities might display one or two of these characteristics, only the traditional cooperative includes all three. As we will see, the *traditional cooperative* is a relatively recent invention, as it was in only comparatively recent times that these characteristics became widely accepted as hallmarks of the cooperative entity.

B. Cooperative Principles

Although the definition already discussed helps us distinguish the cooperative from other business entities, cooperatives and organizations promoting cooperatives have established cooperative principles that further define what cooperatives are and how they function. Most scholars agree that the first set of cooperative principles was developed by the Rochdale Society of

Equitable Pioneers in England in the 1840s. (As discussed later in this chapter, this Society is generally recognized as the first modern cooperative.) The principles developed by this society included open membership, the one-member/one-vote principle, limited return on capital, net savings distributed on the basis of members' use of the cooperative, and support for cooperative education.

Over the years, various organizations including the ICA and the USDA have modified these principles and promulgated new lists of "cooperative principles" in an effort to establish the basic principles that delineate the cooperative and that can be easily taught in the context of cooperative education. Many cooperatives in the United States have adopted some version of the following principles:

- Open membership, which now emphasizes the concept of nondiscriminatory membership
- Democratic control by the cooperative's members, which includes the one-member/one-vote concept for centralized cooperatives, and the concept of democratic representation for federated cooperatives (cooperatives made up of other cooperatives)
- Economic participation by the members on an equitable and democratic basis, where most of the cooperative's capital is the common property of the cooperative, and most "profits" (margins) are distributed to members on the basis of their use of the cooperative, with some set aside for reserves
- Education and training for the cooperative's members, directors, and managers, as well as education for the general public about the nature and benefits of cooperation
- Cooperative autonomy and independence, meaning that if the cooperative enters into agreements or receives assistance from the government or other organizations, it does so only if it ensures the continued independence of the cooperative and the democratic control of its members

Cooperative education is an important, sometimes overlooked, principle that plays an important role both in the success of individual cooperatives and in the overall success of the cooperative business form as a whole. For individual cooperatives, educational programs and materials for members, directors, and managers can assist the cooperative's owners and operators in better understanding their responsibilities as well as the practical application of the cooperative principles. Also, because cooperatives are typically formed by the many rather than the few, educational materials aimed at the general public or at communities most likely to benefit from cooperatives can help individuals understand the cooperative structure and assess whether they could benefit from using the cooperative entity for their business enterprises.

Various public and private organizations assist cooperatives in providing such cooperative education. The USDA provides educational materials and training through its Cooperative Services program and provides funding for cooperative education and development centers across the United States through its rural cooperative development grant program.[5] While in the past the USDA's cooperative assistance has focused on agricultural cooperatives, the USDA has indicated its intent to expand its cooperative programs to include other types of rural cooperatives as well. The USDA's assistance includes helping those interested in forming cooperatives with creating feasibility studies and business plans, offering training for directors, and working with groups of people around the country to help them form cooperatives.

The USDA also provides technical assistance to existing cooperatives on certain issues. Interestingly, the USDA is required by law to provide cooperative education, in that the Cooperative Marketing Act of 1926, which authorized the Secretary of Agriculture to establish a division of cooperative marketing, required the USDA through that division to "promote the knowledge of cooperative principles and practices and cooperate in promoting such knowledge with educational and marketing agencies, cooperative associations, and others."[6]

Cooperative education also includes educating the general public and has come to include lobbying efforts by cooperative groups aimed at state and federal lawmakers and decision makers. Various national cooperative organizations including the National Cooperative Business Association, the National Rural Electric Cooperative Association, and the National Association of Housing Cooperatives, among others, provide funds to initiatives favoring cooperatives and have staff members who serve as legislative representatives.

C. Origin of the Cooperative Form of Business

1. Emergence of the Modern Cooperative

Although there are examples of cooperative endeavors throughout human history, including cooperative tenant farming in ancient Babylonia and burial benefit societies in ancient Greece, cooperatives somewhat resembling modern consumer cooperatives first appeared in Europe in the late 1700s in response to changes brought about by the Industrial Revolution. It was this strand of cooperative development that ultimately resulted in the cooperative principles that most cooperatives follow today.

Before the Industrial Revolution, most people lived outside cities, produced their own food, and made or traded locally for other needed items or services. The employment opportunities offered by the opening of mills and factories drew many working people into or near cities and away from their farms. As this process continued, the workers became consumers rather than producers and purchased food and other products rather than producing such items themselves.

During this period, workers typically worked long hours and often found their wages low in comparison to the prices charged by shops and company stores for food and other necessary items. Also, more than a few storekeepers adopted the practice of adulterating goods by adding fillers to milk, flour, and bread to increase their profits. It was in this environment that groups of workers began pooling their money to buy products from wholesalers of higher quality and at lower prices. These consumer cooperatives purchased food and other items in bulk and made the products available to their members at not much over cost. In a time when food costs were often a family's largest single expense, such cooperatives had the potential to greatly improve the lives of their members.

While the Industrial Revolution brought about consumerism and increased population density, it did not bring any increase in public services or public assistance. Those who were unemployed or sick could not turn to public institutions for help. Other basic services, such as fire and rescue services, were also unavailable. As a result, in times of need, workers had to rely on their own resources or those of their families or neighbors. Perhaps based on the successful example of the new consumer cooperatives, workers began organizing cooperative associations to provide services such as fire insurance and aid in the event of unemployment or sickness.

The formation of cooperative organizations was particularly strong in England. By the early 1800s, a cooperative movement had developed in England, spurred on by individuals interested in forming social cooperatives as well as business cooperatives. Consumer cooperatives were especially popular, and various groups experimented with such cooperatives and went so far as to publish cooperative journals discussing cooperative principles. At this point in time, there was no standardized form or method for forming and operating the cooperative, as well as no law or statute specifically authorizing or governing the cooperative, and a great deal of experimentation occurred.

Most scholars on the subject consider a small cooperative retail store formed near Manchester, England, in 1844 by a group calling themselves the Rochdale Society of Equitable Pioneers to represent the beginning of the modern cooperative era. The group formed what would today be called a consumer cooperative that sold groceries and home goods to its members and, in the process, developed the guiding principles for cooperatives that are still used by most cooperatives in Europe and the United States today. Although previous cooperatives had followed some or all of these principles, the Rochdale Pioneers took the step of combining and codifying these principles and, in doing so, created a model that widely influenced and, to some degree created, the modern cooperative model.

The Rochdale cooperative placed particular emphasis on the principle of democratic control; that is, the principle that all of the cooperative's members vote on matters concerning the cooperative on a one-member/one-vote basis. While over the years other principles have been subject to modification, the democratic nature of the cooperative has come to be understood as a critical, fundamental element of the cooperative. If this element is not present in an organization, many scholars would agree that the organization cannot be classified as a cooperative.

2. Early American Cooperatives

The cooperative movement in America has auspicious roots. Although few cooperatives are recorded during America's colonial period, many sources suggest that Benjamin Franklin was responsible for forming the first successful cooperative organization in the colonies in 1752—a mutual fire insurance cooperative known as the Philadelphia Contributorship for the Insurance of Homes from Loss of Fire. Franklin modeled the cooperative after mutual insurance companies operating in England, and the cooperative insured its members' property against fire, a great threat in towns such as Philadelphia that contained long rows of wooden houses. Franklin's organization is still in operation today. Despite the success of this and other early cooperatives, however, the formation of cooperative organizations in America was limited in scope until the early 1800s.

While consumer cooperatives in England and Europe were beginning to enjoy success in the early 1800s, agricultural cooperatives were beginning to appear in the United States, especially in New England. Although these cooperatives did not have all of the characteristics of the modern cooperative, they were run as cooperatives in practice. One of the first agricultural cooperative organizations in the United States was a creamery established in Connecticut in 1810, while retail milk distribution cooperatives were set up in some cities beginning in the 1820s. Many of these cooperatives ultimately failed because of their uncertain status under federal and state law, since at that time no legislation had been passed providing for such entities. As more Americans moved into the Midwest, agricultural cooperatives began to appear there as well in the early 1800s, including hog marketing cooperatives and manufacturing cooperatives.

Consumer cooperatives were started in the United States beginning in the 1840s, with one cooperative store opening its doors in Boston in 1845. More stores appeared and were eventually operated under the umbrella of the New England Protective Union, which is said to have operated on principles adopted from the Rochdale principles. Other retail and wholesale cooperative organizations opened during this period, although many of these organizations would not meet our working definition of a cooperative. Many of the early cooperative organizations, agricultural, consumer, or otherwise, failed as a result of insufficient capital or poor management. In other cases, cooperative organizations were taken over by groups of members and transformed into for-profit corporations.

Another type of cooperative entity, the savings and loan association, began to enjoy success in America in the 1830s. The first savings and loan association, the Oxford Provident Building Association of Philadelphia, began operation in 1831. Like other financial institutions, the savings and loan association accepted deposits and made loans. Unlike other banks, however, many savings and loan associations were mutually held by their members—depositors and borrowers—who had voting rights and thus played a role in the management of the institution. As a result, savings and loan associations offered services to individuals and small businesses in their communities that were not provided by other financial institutions, which in the early 1800s typically served only the wealthy. Another type of cooperative bank, the mutual savings bank, also has its roots in the early 1800s. Mutual savings banks, which are also owned by their depositors and borrowers, were initially formed by philanthropists working to encourage those in the working classes to save their money and to teach principles of thrift.

Yet another type of cooperative organization, the mutual life insurance company, has its origins in the United States in the 1840s, when the first such company was chartered in New York. A mutual life insurance company is owned by its policyholders, who elect a board of directors to manage the company. Profits from the company are distributed to the policyholders. Many of the early mutual life insurance companies are still in operation today, such as the Northwestern Mutual Life Insurance Company, founded in 1857,[7] and the Massachusetts Mutual Life Company, founded in 1851.[8]

3. Development of Cooperatives After the Civil War

In the period after the Civil War and before 1900, other than cooperatives offering financial and insurance services, the primary growth in cooperatives was among agricultural cooperatives, which will be discussed in a moment. However, other types of cooperatives were developed during this period as well. The first nonagricultural purchasing cooperatives for businesses were formed; for example, a group of small printers in Chicago established a cooperative to purchase supplies in the 1870s, and retail grocers in Baltimore organized a cooperative in the 1880s to buy groceries at wholesale for its members. The first cooperative housing began in New York in the 1880s and consisted of apartment buildings purchased by the entity's stockholders, with individual apartments leased to the stockholders, or, with the consent of the stockholders, to non-stockholders.

After the Civil War, agricultural cooperative organizations received a boost as a result of the activities of an agricultural organization formed in 1867, known as the National Grange, or more simply, the Grange.[9] The

Grange began in reaction to the depressed state of agriculture after the Civil War, and worked to obtain favorable legislation and economic benefits for farmers. The Grange rapidly gained members and at its height in the mid-1870s reportedly had over a million members. Its members began state and local "granges," with many local granges establishing agriculture processing and purchasing cooperatives and consumer and farm supply cooperatives. By some estimates these cooperatives directly or indirectly benefited millions of Americans in the 1870s.

Because leaders of the Grange were familiar with the Rochdale principles and had in fact visited cooperatives in Europe, the Grange published a set of rules for cooperative stores that resulted in many of the local cooperatives being organized and operated on similar principles. Other organizations patterned after the Grange also began cooperative organizations throughout the United States. Although many of these organizations ultimately failed, some were the ancestors of cooperatives still in existence today. The Grange remains in existence and currently has over 300,000 members.

When American industry began to develop with leaps and bounds in the late 1800s, farmers and other small business owners came to realize that to compete in the marketplace, they needed to increase their market power by forming associations of some kind. Farmers found themselves at a disadvantage when attempting to negotiate individually with the new giant corporate entities, such as railroads and equipment manufacturers. Many farmers were especially disadvantaged in dealing with markets and purchasers increasingly owned and controlled by trusts and large corporations. The cooperative form provided to be the most suitable vehicle, and cooperatives quickly gained popularity, especially in agriculture. The Supreme Court of North Carolina summarized the situation as follows in this opinion from 1923:

> The co-operative marketing system was forced into existence to guarantee fair prices to the producer, a fair wage for labor, and to prevent extortion upon the consumer. It increased consumption, by furnishing the consumer a regular supply at less price, and at the same time enabled the laborer and farmer to obtain a remunerative return. In addition, the co-operative system eliminated unnecessary expenses and costs, as well as the enormous speculative profits realized by combinations which had taken control of the entire process between the producer and the consumer.[10]

By some estimates 14,000 agricultural cooperatives were in operation in the United States by the end of 1920, with the vast majority of these cooperatives formed after 1890. Many of today's major agricultural cooperatives were formed during this period, with several still in operation today.

An important development after the Civil War was the passage of the first cooperative enabling statutes by state legislatures. Before such statutes were passed, cooperatives, if they were officially organized at all, were organized under the general statutes providing for organization of commercial organizations, such as corporations. Since such statutes did not apply specifically to cooperatives, the organizers and members operated in uncertainty as to their rights and liabilities under state law. Also, such general statutes contained no safeguards to assure that cooperatives maintained adherence to the cooperative principles.

Some of the cooperative statutes were passed specifically to protect agricultural cooperatives from large trusts and monopolies. A court construing one such statute stated,

> The conditions which gave rise to the act are known of all men. At the time of its enactment, there was but one buyer for the farmers' tobacco. It mattered not how hard he labored, how valuable his soil, or how fine the quality of his crop, he was obliged to accept whatever the buyer might offer. Indeed, in many instances the buyer absolutely refused to examine his crop or make any offer at all. . . . As individuals, the farmers were unable to cope with the situation.[11]

Massachusetts was the first state to enact legislation specifically providing for incorporation of cooperatives, and did so in 1866. The Massachusetts statute provided for the formation of agricultural cooperatives with capital stock. Although the statute was certainly a step in the right direction, it lacked certain features of modern-day cooperative statutes, such as limitations on the amount of shares owned by each member, restrictions on voting rights, and limitations on dividends and margins. Between 1866 and 1900, at least ten other states passed cooperative statutes, with much of the new legislation using the Massachusetts statute as a model.[12] These states included Pennsylvania (1868), Minnesota (1870), Michigan (1875), California (1878), and New Jersey (1884).

During the same time that agricultural cooperatives began to experience rapid growth, concerns about railroad and oil monopolies and large corporate trusts in other industries resulted in the passage by the U.S. Congress of the Sherman Antitrust Act in 1890.[13] Most states enacted antitrust legislation as well. Under these laws the United States (through its agencies) and the states (typically through the office of the state's attorney general) can bring enforcement actions to end practices prohibited under the antitrust laws, such as price fixing, monopolization of trade, and other actions that may harm or eliminate competition.

In a few cases in the early 1900s, agricultural cooperatives were found to be in violation of federal and state antitrust laws, not because the cooperatives engaged in particular acts of anticompetitive activity, but merely because the cooperatives, by their nature, allowed individual farmers to set common prices and engage in common commercial practices. Courts in Iowa and Colorado, among others, upheld antitrust charges by competitors against agricultural cooperatives.[14] In addition, in some states where antitrust laws provided an exemption for agricultural associations, such laws were held to be unconstitutional.

These actions were instigated by competitors, who, faced with the success of cooperative organizations, saw the new antitrust laws as a means by which to diminish the growing influence and scope of agricultural cooperatives. Several courts, faced with such claims by competitors, rejected such antitrust charges, in some cases finding no allegation or evidence that the members of the cooperative attempted to sell their products for greater than their market value.[15] One such court made the following observations in 1921:

> [I]n the last two years . . . there has been a remarkable development of . . . co-operative associations in new fields. Giant marketing associations, covering whole states, or even groups of states, have been organized with startling rapidity in the great cotton and tobacco growing states. . . . These associations have become necessary, not only as a matter of justice, but also as a matter of existence, to the producers of the great staples of the country, and as a protection against the giant combinations of capital which have been taking all the profits, or more, which should have gone to the producers. . . . Naturally the co-operative movement among the farmers has aroused the opposition of the financial combinations, from whose unlimited power in fixing prices the farmers are seeking to free themselves. . . .[16]

As a result of the Sherman Antitrust Act and similar state acts and the ensuing litigation against cooperatives, cooperatives for a time operated under a cloud of legal uncertainty. Fortunately for the cooperative movement, the large growth in numbers of agricultural cooperatives led to a corresponding growth in their allies and political influence. The cooperatives' allies in the U.S. Congress succeeded in passing the Clayton Act[17] in 1914, which included a provision exempting not-for-profit, nonstock agricultural marketing cooperatives from the antitrust laws. The status of capital stock cooperatives was clarified in 1922, when the Capper-Volstead Act[18] was passed and extended the Clayton Act exemption to stock cooperatives.

These two pieces of legislation provided cooperatives with more certainty concerning their business activities and greatly decreased the ability of competitors to cause baseless antitrust charges to be brought against them. However, agricultural cooperatives are not given a blanket exemption from the antitrust laws. When agricultural cooperatives engage in improper anticompetitive behavior, such as coercing nonmembers to do business with the cooperative, acquiring competitors for anticompetitive purposes, or engaging in collective action designed to eliminate competitors, cooperatives can still be found in violation of the antitrust laws.[19]

In addition to the Clayton Act and the Capper-Volstead Act, Congress provided further support for the cooperative movement with the passage of the Farm Loan Act of 1916[20] (providing for the creation of the Federal Land

Bank, a source of credit for agricultural cooperatives), the Cooperative Marketing Act of 1926[21] (authorizing the USDA to provide additional technical and informational support for cooperatives), and the Agricultural Marketing Act of 1929[22] (establishing the Federal Farm Board).

One of the most important pieces of legislation was the Farm Credit Act of 1933,[23] which established Banks for Cooperatives that could provide credit to cooperatives and their members. This legislation and the ensuing assistance to cooperatives helped solidify the cooperative movement and ensure its survival. Because of the strong support for cooperatives during the 1920s and 1930s by the federal government and the establishment of new cooperative financing institutions, this era is sometimes referred to as the American "golden age" of cooperatives.

To some extent the rapid growth of agricultural cooperatives during this period also resulted from periods of excess supply and, especially after World War I, periods of agricultural depression. One court assessed the situation after World War I as follows:

> When the World War ended there was a scarcity amounting almost to destitution in some sections, and in others there was so great an abundance that the producers could not obtain a reasonable living. For the producers of agricultural products the prices were high and there was no profit. . . . Middlemen, speculators, and people who stood between the producers and consumers derived excessive profits from this situation, while the producers and laborers were denied a living. . . . It was the heyday of profiteering.[24]

Forming cooperatives thus can be seen as a defensive reaction to depressed prices and overreaching wholesalers and purchasers. Farmers could lower their costs through joint purchases of supplies, such as feed, tools, and equipment, and could also lower costs of processing, storage, and shipping. It was during this time, for example, that cooperatives were developed to provide services to farmers such as grain storage and grain elevators.

In addition to the advantages offered through increased market power and decreased costs, farmers also saw the marketing advantages offered by cooperatives, such as the ability to develop recognizable brand names for their products. A cooperative could market fungible products provided by its members and create a brand that would draw consumers to the product. For example, the Southern California Fruit Exchange, a marketing cooperative formed in 1893, increased sales by marketing its members' produce under the "Sunkist" label. This example proved a useful model for other cooperatives, which also developed brand names for what had before been commodity products. Marketing cooperatives continued to grow and enjoy success, as shown by later cooperatives such as Blue Diamond Growers, formed in 1910, and Ocean Spray, formed in 1930.

During the early 1900s, a boom also occurred in the formation of organizations to help promote and assist cooperatives and their members. For example, the American Farm Bureau Federation, formed in 1919, provides assistance and advice to farm cooperatives, as well as lobbying for state and federal legislation favorable to cooperatives. Today the state Farm Bureaus offer numerous services to their members, including affordable insurance, banking and real estate services. The National Farmers Union, formed in 1902, provides similar assistance and advice to its members, and today has over 250,000 members.

Organizations such as the Farm Bureau did not spring from the same source or philosophy as the Grange, but out of the new agricultural colleges and a new phenomenon that arose in the early 1900s, the "extension agents" who set forth from such colleges to assist and educate farmers in the field concerning new and improved agricultural methods. These agents eventually formed local and state organizations that evolved into local and state farm bureaus, and then into the national Farm Bureau. Aside from the services that these organizations provided to their members, these organizations had lasting influence through their lobbying efforts. Beginning in the 1920s, a series of federal, state and local acts were passed through the efforts of the national cooperative organizations and members of Congress from southern and Midwestern states, including some of the legislation already discussed.

Aside from the phenomenal growth of agricultural cooperatives, other types of cooperatives also flourished beginning in the early 1900s. Credit unions, which originated in Europe in the 1800s, began in the United States with the formation of the St. Mary's Bank Credit Union of Manchester, New Hampshire, in 1908. In 1934, Congress passed the Federal Credit Union Act,[25] which established the federal credit union system and allowed credit unions to be established under federal or state law. Credit unions enabled many persons to obtain bank accounts and mortgages who otherwise would not have been eligible or financially able to open accounts or obtain mortgages at commercial banks. Today, credit unions offer a wide range of financial products and often offer their members higher interest rates and lower mortgage rates than other financial institutions as a result of their cooperative structure.

Cooperatives received another boost with the election of Franklin Roosevelt and the subsequent passage of federal legislation addressing cooperatives, including the Rural Electrification Act,[26] which aided electric cooperatives, the aforementioned Federal Credit Union Act, and other acts that provided assistance for cooperative housing projects and extended credit for agricultural cooperatives, among other things. One interesting development was the short-lived formation of farmer cooperatives by the government's Farm Security Administration in the late 1930s. During the 1930s farmers were among those hardest hit by the Depression, and after various other programs failed to have any effect, the Farm Security Administration (FSA) was formed to aid poor farmers, in part by providing loans to enable tenant farmers to become landowners and to establish medical clinics. For our purposes, the program of most interest was the FSA's encouragement of the formation of cooperatives by farmers; by some accounts over 16,000 cooperatives were formed with low-income farmers as members. Because of lack of adequate capital caused by the controversial nature of the FSA's programs, as well as lack of training for the cooperatives' managers, most of these cooperatives were short-lived.

Based on the success of agricultural cooperatives, with the assistance of the federal government rural residents formed electric cooperatives to provide power in areas of the country that investor owned cooperatives deemed uneconomical to supply. President Roosevelt signed an executive order in 1935 that created the Rural Electrification Administration (REA),[27] and in 1936, Congress authorized over $400 million for the program and gave REA status as a federal agency within the USDA.[28] The REA provided subsidized loans for the construction of the infrastructure needed to supply power to such areas, and cooperatives were quickly formed to apply for such loans and begin construction.

A similar program was begun in 1949 to accelerate the growth of rural telephone cooperatives. The REA program was one of the most successful initiatives of the New Deal: Immediately before Congress authorized loan funds in 1936, only one out of ten farm families had electric service, while after twenty years, the growth of electric cooperatives resulted in nine out of ten farm families having electricity. The REA has since been transformed into the Rural Utilities Service, and continues to assist electric and telephone cooperatives today.

One modern major development has been the growth in retailer cooperatives; that is, retailer owned purchasing cooperatives that purchase goods and services on behalf of their business members, which might or might not be cooperatives themselves. Retailer cooperatives have been particularly successful among grocery stores, pharmacies, and hardware stores, and include major businesses such as Ace Hardware, whose members are local hardware stores.

Other modern cooperatives have developed in reaction to changes in lifestyle, such as automobile sharing cooperatives, in which the cooperative purchases automobiles and makes them available on demand to members for low hourly or daily fees. Automobile sharing cooperatives have recently increased in popularity as consumers face increasing costs in maintaining privately owned automobiles and increasingly congested roads. In some cases changing demographics have aided cooperative growth as well. For example, because of the rising number of retired persons, in several states, retirees have banded together to form cooperative retirement communities in which retirees can more effectively control costs and ensure excellent care.

Also, in some cases, states have provided support for the formation of certain types of cooperatives to encourage endeavors that would otherwise be unprofitable. Certain states including West Virginia and Kentucky have assisted cooperatives that allow their members to produce art and handicrafts in their homes in rural areas to supplement their income. Some of these cooperatives have opened retail outlets, managed by the members, to provide an outlet for members' products.

4. New Types of Cooperatives

The cooperative model has demonstrated its flexibility by continuing to change to adapt to changing business conditions. In the 1980s and 1990s, farmers were faced with falling commodity prices and saw commodity processors receive rising profits. Commodity processors purchased the raw commodities from farmers, such as corn and wheat, and added value (and received increasing profits) by processing the commodities into retail products, such as ethanol or pasta. Farmers wanted to obtain a greater share of the consumer's dollar by having their cooperatives control more stages of the commodity's progress to the consumer's shopping cart. However, farmers found that limitations of existing marketing cooperatives made it difficult to achieve such a transition. In particular, expanding into commodity processing required tremendous amounts of capital to purchase the necessary equipment, and the traditional marketing cooperative was not suited to quickly obtain such capital from its members or from outside investors.

Because the traditional cooperative has a limited return on investment and restrictions on transferring ownership, the traditional cooperative typically receives no equity capital from nonmembers and only gradually receives capital from its members. (Capitalization and financing of cooperatives is discussed in detail in Chapter VI.) Confronted with these challenges, some cooperatives converted into a different form of business entity, typically a limited liability company (LLC), and some new ventures chose a form of entity other than the cooperative. However, others modified the traditional marketing cooperative form to accommodate the need for larger and faster infusions of capital. Although the resulting model has been given different names, including "new age cooperative" and "value added cooperative," such cooperatives are referred to as "new generation cooperatives" in this book.

As with cooperatives in general, new generation cooperatives were developed in reaction to a particular set of circumstances: Farmers wanted to vertically integrate their cooperatives through adding processing, manufacturing, and wholesale/retail functions, but they could not obtain adequate financing through the traditional cooperative structure. Although there are variances among new generation cooperatives, particularly in light of the differing state statutes that might govern their organization, most new generation cooperatives share certain core characteristics:

- The requirement of a substantial equity investment in the cooperative from each member. This differs from the traditional cooperative in which capital is primarily obtained through retained earnings.

- Contractually fixed delivery rights and obligations of members to deliver a specified quantity and quality of products to the cooperative. Delivery rights are based on the member's equity contribution to the new generation cooperative and are represented by equity shares in the new generation cooperative. In the traditional cooperative, members can deliver as much or as little to the cooperative as they choose.
- A closed membership in which a limited number of members are admitted. This characteristic is a natural consequence of having fixed delivery rights. In the traditional cooperative, membership is open.
- Fewer restrictions on transferability of rights and interests in the new generation cooperative among members. In some new generation cooperatives, shares are freely transferable among existing members, which, together with the fact that shares are tied to market rights, means that shares can increase and decrease in value. Shares in traditional cooperatives are typically difficult to transfer and are not marketable.

Despite these and other differences, most new generation cooperatives still retain the primary characteristics of the traditional cooperative, such as the requirements that a majority of shares be owned by producers, rather than investors, that each producer member has one vote, and that dividends be limited to no more than eight percent. In fact, new generation cooperatives, which first gained popularity in the 1970s, were initially organized under existing cooperative statutes. However, the growth of new generation cooperatives has been spurred by the passage of state legislation that specifically recognizes and allows for the special features of new generation cooperatives, and beginning in the 1990s, several states, including Iowa, Wyoming, Wisconsin, Minnesota, and Tennessee, passed statutes authorizing the creation of cooperative business structures incorporating the elements discussed.[29] In some cases, the statutes were applicable only to agricultural cooperatives; in others, the statutes had more general application. These new statutes grant a considerable amount of flexibility. For example, some statutes allow the organization to grant a majority of voting rights in non-patron members, to direct a majority of the earnings to non-patron members on the basis of investment, or to exceed the eight percent dividend limit applicable to traditional cooperatives. Cooperatives organized under these statutes may elect to be taxed as either corporations or partnerships. These statutes still protect patron-member interests to varying degrees, such as by requiring that a majority of directors be elected by patron members or by setting a minimum allocation of earnings to patron members.

These statutes combine elements of the traditional cooperative with attributes of unincorporated associations such as LLCs. However, the various statutes lacked uniformity, and some were aimed primarily at agricultural cooperatives. In recognition of the new cooperative statutes and the need for a cooperative model that provided greater flexibility in obtaining outside investments, the National Conference of Commissioners on Uniform State Laws (NCCUSL) developed a uniform law that was ultimately recommended to the states for adoption in 2007: the Uniform Limited Cooperative Association Act (LCAA).[30] As with the statutes already discussed, the LCAA was not intended to replace traditional cooperative statutes, but to provide an alternative to entities that sought to combine use of the cooperative principles with the ability to attract equity investment from outside investors.

The LCAA provides for the formation of "limited cooperative associations," which are unincorporated associations that combine cooperative principles with certain aspects of LLCs The LCAA allows limited cooperative associations to have investor members with voting rights in addition to patron members, and thus allows greater opportunities for obtaining equity investors. The LCAA is intended to allow sufficient flexibility so that limited cooperative associations can make use of the features found in "new age cooperatives," while at the same time ensuring that such associations retain traditional cooperative principles. The latter point is of particular importance since cooperative ventures organized under other organizational statutes, such as LLC statutes, do not necessarily adhere closely to the cooperative principles.[31]

The LCAA is also designed for use by nonagricultural cooperatives. The NCCUSL states that the LCAA "contemplates the formation of various types of limited cooperative associations, including marketing, advertising, bargaining, processing, purchasing, real estate, and worker owned cooperatives," and could be used, for example, "by an urban food cooperative to attract investment capital to build facilities for the operation of the cooperative's business."[32] It is entirely possible, and certainly to be hoped for, that enactment of the LCAA by the states will encourage the development of a new crop of cooperatives.

The emergence of new cooperative forms, such as the new generation cooperative and the limited cooperative association, has not occurred without debate. Some commentators question whether or to what extent such organizations are "cooperatives." However, a consistent theme in the development of the cooperative form has been adaptation to changing conditions, and cooperatives have often been developed in reaction to adverse circumstances, such as depressed markets, a lack of affordable alternatives, or overreaching suppliers and purchasers. From this perspective, it is not surprising that the cooperative business model continues to develop new branches.

Notes

1. Frost v. Corp. Comm'n of State of Okla., 278 U.S. 515, 546 (1929) (Brandeis, J., dissenting).

2. Donald A. Frederick, *Co-ops 101: An Introduction to Cooperatives*, USDA COOPERATIVE INFORMATION REPORT NO. 55, 1 (1997).
3. Report of the International Co-operative Alliance Commission on Co-operative Principles (1966).
4. *See* Galen Rapp & Gerald Ely, *How to Start a Cooperative*, USDA COOPERATIVE INFORMATION REPORT NO. 7, *available at* http://www.rurdev.usda.gov/rbs/pub/cir7/cir7.pdf.
5. *See* http://www.rurdev.usda.gov/rbs/coops/csdir.htm.
6. Cooperative Marketing Act of 1926, 44 Stat. 802, 802.
7. http://www.nmfn.com/tn/learnctr—nm_hist_timeline.
8. http://www.massmutual.com/mmfg/about/ourstory/index.html.
9. http://www.nationalgrange.org/about/history.html.
10. Tobacco Growers Co-operative Ass'n v. Jones, 117 S.E. 174, 179 (N.C. 1923).
11. Commonwealth v. Hodges, 125 S.W. 689 (Ky. App. 1910). *See also Tobacco Growers' Co-operative Ass'n*, 117 S.E. at 179.
12. Frost v. Corp. Comm'n of State of Okla., 278 U.S. at 539 (Brandeis, J., dissenting).
13. Sherman Act, ch. 647, 26 Stat. 209 (1890) (codified as amended at 15 U.S.C. §§ 1–7 (2000 & Supp. 2004)).
14. *See, e.g.*, Burns v. Wray Farmers' Grain Co., 176 P. 487 (Colo. 1918); Reeves v. Decorah Farmers' Co-operative Soc'y, 140 N.W. 844 (Iowa 1913).
15. Tobacco Growers' Co-operative Ass'n v. Jones, 117 S.E. 174 (N.C. 1923); Burley Tobacco Soc'y v. Gillaspy, 100 N.E. 89 (Ind. App. 1912).
16. *Tobacco Growers' Co-operative Ass'n*, 117 S.E. at 182.
17. Clayton Act, ch. 323, 38 Stat. 730 (1914) (codified as amended at 15 U.S.C. §§ 12–27 (2000 & Supp. 2004), 29 U.S.C. §§ 52–53 (2000)).
18. Capper-Volstead Act of 1922, ch. 57, 42 Stat. 388 (codified as amended at 7 U.S.C. §§ 291–292 (1994 & Supp. 1999)).
19. *See, e.g.*, Md. & Va. Milk Producers Ass'n v. United States, 362 U.S. 458, 468 (1960).
20. Federal Farm Act of 1916, Pub. L. No. 64-158, 39 Stat. 360 (codified as amended at 12 U.S.C. § 672 (1988)).
21. Cooperative Marketing Act of 1926, ch. 725, §§ 1–7, 44 Stat. 802 (codified as amended at 7 U.S.C. §§ 451–457 (1983)).
22. Agricultural Marketing Act, ch. 24, § 1, 46 Stat. 11 (1929) (repealed 1933).
23. Farm Credit Act of 1933, Pub. L. No. 73-76, 48 Stat. 257, 259 (repealed 1953).
24. *Tobacco Growers' Co-operative Ass'n*, 117 S.E. at 179.
25. Federal Credit Union Act, Pub. L. No. 73-467, § 9, 48 Stat. 1216, 1219 (codified as amended at 12 U.S.C. § 1759 (1994)).
26. Rural Electrification Act of 1936, Pub. L. No. 74-605, 49 Stat. 1363 (codified as amended at 7 U.S.C. §§ 901-18 (2006)).
27. Exec. Order No. 7,037 (May 11, 1935) (uncodified).
28. Rural Electrification Act of 1936, *supra* note 26.
29. *See, e.g.*, Iowa Code Ann. §§ 501A.101 to 501A.1216; Minn. Stat. Ann. §§ 308B.001 to 308B.975; Tenn. Code Ann. §§ 43-38-101 to 43-38-1109; Wyo. Stat. Ann. §§ 17-10-201 to 17-10-253; Wis. Stat. Ann. §§ 193.001 to 193.971.
30. Uniform Limited Cooperative Association Act (2007), *available at* http://www.law.upenn.edu/bll/archives/ulc/uaarca/2007_final.htm.

31. For further background on the development of the LCAA, see The Uniform Limited Cooperative Association Act: An Introduction, by Thomas E. Geu, Reporter for the LCAA and James B. Dean, Associate Reporter for the LCAA (Oct. 2007), *available at* http://www.nccusl.org/Update/Docs/AALACooperativePaperOctober2007FINAL.doc.; and the prefatory note and comments to the LCAA, *available at* http://www.law.upenn.edu/bll/archives/ulc/uaarca/2007_final.htm.

32. *Why States Should Adopt the Uniform Limited Cooperative Association Act*, THE NATIONAL CONFERENCE OF COMMISSIONERS ON UNIFORM STATE LAWS, *available at* http://www.nccusl.org/Update/uniformact_why/uniformacts-why-ULCAA.asp.

Further Reading

For more information about the cooperative principles, see *Cooperative Business Principles*, USDA COOPERATIVE INFORMATION REPORT No. 45, Section 2 (1994); Ann Hoyt, *And Then There Were Seven: Cooperative Principles Updated*, UNIVERSITY OF WISCONSIN CENTER FOR COOPERATIVES, COOPERATIVE GROCER, Jan./Feb. 1996, *available at* www.uwcc.wisc.edu/staff/hoyt/princart.html.

For additional information on the historical development of the cooperative form, see JOHN HANNA, THE LAW OF COOPERATIVE MARKETING ASSOCIATIONS (1931), and ISRAEL PACKEL, THE LAW OF COOPERATIVES (3d ed. 1956).

For an interesting look at the historical development of the cooperative form in countries other than the United States, see B.J. SURRIDGE & MARGARET DIGBY, A MANUAL OF CO-OPERATIVE LAW AND PRACTICE, (3d ed. 1967).

For more information about the Farm Security Administration, see SIDNEY BALDWIN, POVERTY AND POLITICS: THE RISE AND DECLINE OF THE FARM SECURITY ADMINISTRATION (1968).

For a comparison of traditional cooperatives and new generation cooperatives, see David Coltrain, David Barton & Michael Boland, *Differences Between New Generation Cooperatives and Traditional Cooperatives*, ARTHUR CAPPER COOPERATIVE CENTER (May 2000).

For further information about new generation cooperatives, see Michael L. Cook & Constantine Iliopoulos, *Beginning to Inform the Theory of the Cooperative Firm: Emergence of the New Generation Cooperative*, FINNISH JOURNAL OF BUSINESS ECONOMICS (April 1999); and Randall E. Torgeson, *A Critical Look at New Generation Cooperatives*, RURAL COOPERATIVES MAGAZINE, Jan./Feb. 2001, *available at* www.rurdev.usda.gov/rbs/pub/jan01/critical.htm.

For an interesting discussion of the "new generation cooperative" state statutes and some of the cooperatives formed under them, see Lynn Pitman, *Limited Cooperative Association Statutes: An Update*, UNIVERSITY OF WISCONSIN CENTER FOR COOPERATIVES, STAFF PAPER No. 7, April 2008, *available at* http://www.uwcc.wisc.edu/info/uwcc_pubs/staff/staff08.pdf.

For a detailed review of the effect of new cooperative statutes on cooperative finance and governance, see James R. Baarda, *Current Issues in Cooperative Finance and Governance*, USDA RURAL DEVELOPMENT, COOPERATIVE PROGRAMS (April 2006), *available at* http://uwcc.wisc.edu/info/governance/baard.pdf.

III

Using the Cooperative Form of Business

One of the more complex tasks of the business lawyer lies in advising the client on what kind of business structure to use for his or her new business. The cooperative, just like any other business structure, is suitable for some business enterprises and not for others. While the decision whether to use a corporation, a limited liability company (LLC) or a limited partnership is typically based solely on economic and legal considerations, the decision whether to use the cooperative form often involves social and political factors as well. One reason for this difference lies in the cooperative's primary focus on providing benefits for its members, rather than on providing profits for investors. Whether to use the cooperative form also depends at least in part on the line of business the enterprise will pursue, since for certain business pursuits the cooperative entity can obtain advantages through special tax treatment, government programs aimed at assisting cooperatives, and low-interest loans and government-backed loan guarantees.

Also, while corporations, LLCs, and other business entities are typically formed to market new products or take advantage of market opportunities, cooperatives are often formed in reaction to market events, such as the formation of monopolies in certain industries, rising prices of necessary products or services, or the inability to obtain certain goods and services in a geographic market. For example, the failure of investor-owned electric power companies to provide electric service to most of rural America led to the formation and growth of rural electric cooperatives in the 1930s and 1940s, with such cooperatives receiving guidance and financial assistance from the Rural Electrification Administration, a government agency.

If the founders of an enterprise decide that the cooperative is the preferable business structure, how is the cooperative formed? In many states corporations, LLCs and other entities can be formed online in a matter of minutes using menu-driven systems, user-created forms, and credit card payments.

Certainly most attorneys are familiar with the basic requirements for creating these entities, and many bookstores also carry numerous books aimed at helping entrepreneurs do it themselves. Forming the cooperative is more challenging, since in many states there may be multiple statutes providing for formation. Making formation even more interesting, some states now have new statutory schemes that allow for creation of the new generation cooperatives and limited cooperative associations discussed in Chapter II.

Once the task of filing the organizational documents is completed, the more complex task of drafting the bylaws and related documents must be accomplished. "Off the shelf" documents are usually not available, since documents such as the bylaws must be tailor-made to coordinate with the applicable state statutory scheme and with the interests and needs of the cooperative's members. The complexity of the cooperative's bylaws will depend on the cooperative's line of business, as well as the type of cooperative involved. For example, a federated cooperative made up of other cooperatives will likely require a sophisticated set of bylaws.

This chapter will first compare and contrast the cooperative with other types of business entities. Next to be examined will be the decision-making process involved in determining when it is appropriate to use the cooperative form. Finally, this chapter will discuss the formation of the cooperative and will consider some of the issues involved in drafting the cooperative's organizational documents.

A. Comparison of the Cooperative Entity With Other Business Entities

The best way to truly understand the unique features of the cooperative is to compare the cooperative with other types of business entities. If one examined cooperative structure through the contents of traditional state cooperative acts, one would be struck by the surface similarities between cooperatives and corporations. For example,

- Both the owner/members of the cooperative and the shareholders of the corporation have limited liability; that is, there is no personal liability for the debts and obligations incurred by the cooperative or the corporation.
- Both cooperatives and corporations have perpetual existence.
- Cooperatives, like corporations, are typically formed through the filing of articles of incorporation and usually adopt bylaws to govern operations.
- Like corporations, cooperatives have officers and elected boards of directors.
- Cooperatives employ accounting systems similar to those employed by corporations.

- The standard of care owed by the cooperative's officers and directors to the cooperative is very similar to the standard of care applicable to corporate officers and directors.

Many of these similarities are of relatively recent origin and came about through the fact that many state cooperative statutes were based on, or borrowed liberally from, state corporation statutes. Many traditional cooperatives thus have the trappings of corporations.

Cooperatives can be formed using unincorporated structures as well. For example, even where a state cooperative act is available, the state's LLC act or limited liability partnership act can be used to organize an entity with cooperative attributes. Also, as discussed in Chapter II, limited cooperative associations formed under modern state statutes based on the Uniform Limited Cooperative Association Act are unincorporated entities for state law purposes. In fact, limited cooperative associations share attributes of both unincorporated and incorporated entities, since their organizational documents are modeled on corporate law.

Let us now turn to the differences between traditional cooperatives and other types of business entities.

1. Return on Investment and Financing Techniques

Owners of for-profit companies anticipate a return on their investment. In essence, owners expect a return for the risk they incur in speculating, in the form of their investment, on the success of the company. In contrast, the member/owners of the traditional cooperative do not receive a direct return in exchange for their risk in investing in the cooperative. This is because the cooperative is intended to operate essentially at cost for the benefit of its members/owners. Although the cooperative can, and typically does, generate profits (typically referred to as "margins") and can use some of these profits for necessary reserves and for achieving growth of the entity, most profits are returned to the members on a periodic basis in the form of patronage refunds. Because the amount of the patronage refund is based on the member's use of the cooperative (e.g., through purchases from or sales to the cooperative), rather than the size of the member's ownership interest, the refund does not represent a "return on investment," but is intended to return benefits of the cooperative to the members.

As one might expect, financing of the cooperative is also different than for other business entities. For traditional cooperatives, state laws and/or the cooperative's bylaws typically prohibit the sale or transfer of common stock (for stock cooperatives) or membership interests (for nonstock cooperatives) to nonmembers. (For a comparison of stock cooperatives and nonstock cooperatives, see Chapter IV.) Although in some cases the cooperative can sell preferred stock to nonmembers that pays a specified dividend, such preferred stock carries no voting rights and the amount of the dividend is subject to restrictions under federal and state law. In any event, relatively few cooperatives actually sell preferred stock. As a result, the traditional cooperative usually lacks outside investors, especially during the early life of the cooperative, and relies primarily on debt financing for its capital expenditures, particularly for fixed assets such as land, buildings and equipment.

Another characteristic of the cooperative also reduces the likelihood of raising capital from outside investors. In the traditional cooperative, a member's shares or membership in the cooperative typically can only be transferred to another member. Even member-to-member transfers often require the approval of the cooperative's board of directors. In some cases these restrictions apply to the transfer of preferred shares and capital certificates as well. For these reasons, for most members of cooperatives there is no market for their shares. Restrictions on sales of preferred stock also limit the market for preferred shares, and essentially cause the value of preferred stock to arise solely from its dividend yield.

The natural question that arises is whether equity capital raised from the cooperative's members could be used in place of debt financing. The answer is that in the traditional cooperative, members typically make only small capital contributions. New members are typically asked to pay a membership fee or (in stock cooperatives) to buy shares of stock for a nominal amount, such as $250. The amount raised in this way is obviously insufficient to provide the necessary capital for the cooperative. Additional capital contributions are, in fact, made by the members during the life of the cooperative, since cooperatives often retain part of their net earnings every year. Because the retained amounts would ordinarily be returned to the members as patronage refunds, these amounts represent equity investments by the members, and are credited to the members' capital accounts in the cooperatives' accounting system. Once again, however, these contributions are made over time, and do not solve the problem of raising sufficient start-up capital. In some cases, the initial equity contributions raised from the members are not sufficient to provide operating capital, and short-term financing must be obtained. (Financing of cooperatives is discussed in Chapter VI.)

The financing of new generation cooperatives shares characteristics of traditional cooperatives and of for-profit corporations. The new member's initial equity investment is typically substantial, and the shares purchased by the new member often represent a binding obligation of the member to provide a specified amount of the commodity marketed or processed by the cooperative. As a result, the cooperative has sufficient funds and contract rights to invest the capital required to purchase factories, processing equipment, and other materials required for a vertically integrated enterprise. Because a member's ownership of stock essentially entitles the member to certain financial rights, cooperative stock has value, and thus a market exists among members for buying and selling shares in the cooperative.

Also, new generation cooperatives typically have fewer restrictions on transferability of shares among members than do traditional cooperatives. In some cases, new generation cooperatives allow outside investors to purchase dividend-bearing preferred stock in the cooperative that does not carry voting rights. In other cases, two classes of membership exist, and non-patron members receive limited voting rights and are allocated distributions proportionate to their investment. Incidentally, the sale of stock to outside investors also provides a way for influential members of the local community to provide economic and political support for the cooperative even when the members are not producers of the particular commodity involved.

As we have seen, both traditional cooperatives and new generation cooperatives are different from other business entities as far as the owners' financial motives and the capitalization of the enterprise. In general, these differences mean that cooperatives can rely less on investors outside the cooperative, and must place more reliance on debt financing or, in the case of new generation cooperatives, on capital contributions from members. However, because favorable debt financing is often available to cooperatives through government programs and cooperative financial institutions, such differences are not necessarily detrimental. In any event, these differences are not surprising in light of the cooperative's emphasis on providing benefits to member/customers, rather than outside investors.

2. Business Purpose, Ownership and Control, and Distribution of Income

Although cooperatives operate in business sectors alongside for-profit corporations, LLCs, and other business entities, cooperatives are often formed for different reasons than their competitors. The founders of a for-profit corporation, LLC, or limited partnership typically envision a business enterprise that will generate profits for the founders and investors. The enterprise is usually started because the founders developed a new product or service, saw a gap in the market that their enterprise could fill, or found an opportunity to provide products or services at a lower price or in larger quantities than currently available in the marketplace. In contrast, cooperatives are often formed for defensive reasons. In gathering together and deciding to form a cooperative, the founders might have been reacting to the inability to obtain needed goods or services in their geographic area, the monopolization of goods or services by a larger company, or rising prices of necessary goods or services.

Although many early cooperatives were formed for defensive reasons, in recent times cooperatives have been formed for proactive reasons as well, such as enabling growers of a commodity, such as wheat, to also process the commodities into finished products and market such products in the marketplace. However, investigation might show that even these cooperatives had their beginning in reaction to a market event, such as the closure of processing plants in the geographic region or decreasing prices for the individual producers' commodities. It makes sense that many cooperatives are formed in reaction to events, since group action is needed to form a cooperative, and larger groups tend to coalesce in reaction to special events or circumstances.

Cooperatives also differ from other business entities in their ownership and control. The cooperative is unlike any other business entity in that its customers also own and control the business. In a small cooperative, it might be possible for all of its members/owners to gather together periodically and participate in managing the cooperative and directing its operations. In practice, although the members/owners have ultimate control over the cooperative, in most instances they delegate their authority to a board of directors that manages the affairs of the cooperative. Typically, the membership of voting directors on the board is restricted by state law and by the cooperative's bylaws to members of the cooperative, although in some cases, larger cooperatives have outside directors on their boards as well. Such outside directors allow the cooperative to acquire specialized expertise that might not be available from its own members, and provide the board with an objective viewpoint as it attempts to balance the sometimes competing interests of various groups of members.

As with the corporation, the cooperative's board of directors almost always hires a manager to run the day-to-day operations of the cooperative. In the cooperative world, the manager typically is the most influential person in steering the course of the cooperative and makes most key business decisions. However, because the members of the board are also members and customers of the cooperative, more than a few cooperatives have strong boards that are heavily involved in the strategic planning of the cooperative and that may require managers to seek advice on matters that the chief executive officer (CEO) of a typical corporation would consider a day-to-day function.

So far, the role of the cooperative's board of directors sounds very similar to the board's role in the corporation. However, the cooperative's owner/member/customer structure differentiates its board from the board of a corporation. In the case of the for-profit corporation, the board of directors is ultimately answerable to the owners. In smaller entities, the two groups may be synonymous; in larger entities, the shareholders typically are satisfied with the board of directors as long as the entity is profitable and continues to grow. The entity's customers, unless they are also shareholders, have no direct influence on the board, and are not taken into consideration (at least in a political sense) for purposes of formulating policies and directing the course of the business.

The cooperative's board faces a much different political landscape, in that the members that elect the board are also the cooperative's customers. The board as a practical matter must satisfy not only the cooperative's owners, but its customers as well. As a result, for the membership to be satisfied with its board, it is not enough for the cooperative to be on a sound footing financially; the cooperative must also fulfill the customers' objectives, which might include providing a certain level of services, providing help to the community, and offering additional services or products desired by the customers. Such intangible objectives are not always compatible with increasing the cooperative's margins (profits) or paying down debt, and the board thus must carefully consider the cooperative's goals and purposes as well as its financial footing in making decisions. The nature of the relationship between the board and the cooperative's membership obviously increases the importance of maintaining communications with the members and providing periodic updates of changes in cooperative initiatives and programs. In some respects a cooperative can be thought of as a political entity pursuing a business objective.

Another key difference to take into account when considering the governance of the cooperative is the one-member/one-vote principle of the cooperative. Typically, every member in the cooperative is entitled to one vote in voting on the cooperative's board of directors and in voting on decisions that require the consent of the members. Although most corporations and LLCs could adopt this governance model if they wished, in the typical corporation and LLC, shareholders and interest holders are given voting rights in proportion to their interest; that is, their investment in the entity. In the typical corporation, then, a major investor will have considerable say in shaping the operations and policies of the corporation, and smaller investors may well be "along for the ride" in terms of control.

In the cooperative, on the other hand, large and small customers alike each have one vote, and thus even the largest customer is unable on its own to block the decision of the majority. From a practical standpoint, while the CEO and board of a corporation might have to consider and obtain the consent of only a relatively small number of shareholders, the manager and board of a cooperative might face a much more politically demanding task in obtaining consensus among the members and in navigating among the various voting blocks that cooperative members invariably form. As discussed in more detail in the following, the practical effects of the one-member/one-vote principle demand careful attention when drafting the cooperative's bylaws.

3. Taxation

One of the primary differences between cooperatives and other business entities concerns their treatment under tax laws, particularly the federal tax laws. Although the tax treatment of cooperatives will be discussed more thoroughly in Chapter VII, including the tax advantages enjoyed by certain kinds of cooperatives, a few key differences are worth noting now.

The federal and state tax laws related to most cooperatives feature certain disincentives for outside investors and for members seeking greater returns on equity contributions. While other entities typically are not restricted as to the amount of dividends they can pay to investors, most state cooperative statutes limit stock dividends to eight percent for agricultural cooperatives. Similarly, federal tax law restricts their dividend rate to the greater of the legal rate permitted in the cooperative's state of incorporation, or eight percent annually. Most other types of cooperatives do not receive a deduction for capital stock dividends, potentially leaving some patronage income subject to double taxation. Other restrictions require profit distributions to be proportionate to patronage. In addition, substantially all stock issued by agricultural cooperatives (except for certain nonvoting preferred stock) must be owned by the cooperatives' patrons.

As one might imagine, these restrictions make it difficult for cooperatives to attract outside equity, especially as compared with other types of entities, such as LLCs. When large amounts of capital are needed, some cooperatives have tackled this problem indirectly by entering into joint ventures with corporations and LLCs. Beginning in the 1980s, cooperatives sought a more direct solution by lobbying for state legislation permitting the formation of "hybrid" cooperatives combining certain features of the traditional cooperative and of the LLC. These statutes are designed to provide the ability for cooperatives that need substantial start-up capital, such as processing cooperatives, to have greater access to non-patron capital. As discussed in Chapter II, several states have passed such statutes, and additional states will likely adopt the Uniform Limited Cooperative Association Act that provides for the formation of limited cooperative associations.

Cooperatives also differ from other entities in that certain restrictions exist on income derived from nonmembers of the cooperative. For example, for certain kinds of cooperatives to maintain their tax exempt status, including electric and telephone cooperatives, such cooperatives must collect at least eighty-five percent of their income from members, subject to certain exceptions. Also, certain kinds of cooperatives otherwise exempt from business income taxes can be taxed on income generated from lines of business unrelated to their central purpose. Both of these restrictions are discussed in more detail in Chapter VII.

B. When to Use the Cooperative Form

As we have seen, the cooperative entity is distinctly different from other types of business entities. The nature of these differences makes the cooperative perfectly suited for use with some types of business enterprises, while at the same time rendering it a very implausible alternative for other enterprises. The most distinctive feature of the cooperative, the union of ownership, control, and patronage, results in the founders of the enterprise considering not only legal and economic factors in deciding whether to use the cooperative form of business, but social and political considerations as well. Unlike the corporation and LLC, in which the business owners do not necessarily have to see eye to eye provided that there are sufficient customers and profits, in the cooperative, especially during the formation period, a comparatively sizeable group of people, many from the same community, will have to agree on major decisions concerning the enterprise. Keeping this example in mind, what other factors play a part in the decision of whether to use the cooperative form, and for what kinds of enterprise is the cooperative form most suitable?

Certain features of the cooperative may be viewed either as advantages for the business form or as neutral factors that do not rule out the cooperative as a possibility. These features include the following:

- A built-in customer base for the business from the beginning of the enterprise.
- Limited ability to provide goods and services outside the core business of the cooperative.
- Depending on the cooperative's line of business, various tax advantages that may enable the cooperative to retain more surplus earnings for growth.
- A group of directors and managers with strong incentives to promote the success of the enterprise, since the directors and managers are not only owners and customers of the cooperative, but are also typically leaders in the local community with social ties to the cooperative's other members.
- Once again depending on the cooperative's line of business, possible access to favorable financing through state and federal guarantees or loans.
- Possible assistance from federal and state programs in the establishment of the cooperative and the training of officers and directors.

Certain other features may pose disadvantages, depending on the line of business the enterprise seeks to enter. These features include the following:

- For traditional cooperatives, legal and practical restrictions on obtaining equity investment from non-patrons.
- For certain kinds of cooperatives, restrictions on payment of dividends and distributions.
- For certain kinds of cooperatives, restrictions on selling goods or providing services to non-members, or, in some cases, from selling goods or providing services outside the core goods and services provided by the cooperative.
- As a function of the requirement for member approval of key decisions, a longer decision-making process for certain decisions of the enterprise.
- In the traditional cooperative, difficulty in economic forecasting because of the freedom of the members to obtain goods from or provide goods to competitors of the cooperative.

Although the effects of some of these factors, especially the advantageous ones, are obvious and require no further explication, others are more subtle and are discussed in more detail in the following.

1. Restrictions on Lines of Business

Cooperatives typically are formed to accomplish a single purpose, such as providing electric power in rural areas, providing financial services to their members, or providing a more affordable way for persons in the same line of business to purchase necessary goods and services, such as farm supplies or insurance. As a practical matter, many cooperatives tend to remain close to their original business purpose, since the expertise of the cooperative's owners lies in the original line of business. The owners intended the cooperative to provide a particular function and may not be interested in expanding the cooperative into other fields of which they have no knowledge or experience.

Cooperatives also stay within their original business purpose because of legal requirements and restrictions. For example, state statutes permitting the organization of certain types of cooperatives, such as electric cooperatives and telephone cooperatives, may restrict cooperatives formed under those statutes from engaging in lines of business not directly related to the cooperative's original purpose. Even if the state does not enforce such laws, expanding into other lines of business could result, and at times has resulted, in expensive legal challenges to the cooperative brought by existing businesses in the new industry.

Tax laws can also affect cooperatives' ability to provide multiple lines of business. For certain kinds of cooperatives to maintain their tax exempt status, such cooperatives may not generate more than an insubstantial amount of income that is not related to their primary function. In addition, certain kinds of cooperatives face taxes on income generated from lines of business unrelated to their central purpose.

For all of these reasons, the cooperative form typically is best suited for an enterprise that will pursue a single line of business or closely related lines of business. If the enterprise intends to grow lines of business wherever the money flows, another form will likely be preferable. If, however, the founders envision providing various types of goods and services to the same group of people, it could be that while the cooperative form is suitable, multiple cooperatives will need to be formed to avoid the practical and legal impediments already discussed. For example, if a group of small businesspeople in a region wanted to form a business entity that would provide insurance services for the members as well as procure needed business supplies for the members, two separate cooperatives would likely be required, both to meet legal requirements and to provide for separate management for each of the cooperatives with skills suited for each line of business.

2. Restrictions on Outside Investment and Payment of Dividends

Cooperatives are sometimes at a disadvantage vis-à-vis other types of business entities in attracting outside investors and raising capital. While corporations and LLCs can attract investors through the potential rewards of dividends and distributions, many cooperatives are restricted in their ability to pay dividends, and because most of the cooperative's profits are returned to members as patronage refunds on the basis of patronage (as discussed in Chapter VI), the lure of increasing profits does not beckon outside investors. Also, while corporations and LLCs can grant outside investors voting rights or give investors a certain number of seats on the board of directors, cooperatives generally cannot give investors any voting rights within the cooperative, and investors, as nonmembers, typically cannot sit on the cooperative's board.

Although cooperatives can obtain limited investment from nonmembers, the traditional cooperative structure is not the most suitable structure for businesses that envision obtaining a sizeable percentage of their financing from outside investors. This conclusion is perhaps intuitive, since cooperatives by their nature are formed for the benefit of their members, and are not designed to be a profit mechanism for those who do not use their services.

As discussed earlier in this chapter, many "new generation cooperatives" are organized under state statutes that allow such cooperatives greater flexibility in selling preferred stock to outside investors. In some cases, such cooperatives are allowed to have two classes of members, with one class consisting of non-patron investors who received certain voting rights and financial return proportionate to investment. Also, in the coming years, as states adopt the Uniform Limited Cooperative Association Act, limited cooperative associations will be formed that share many of the characteristics of new generation cooperatives and that will also have the ability to attract equity investment from outside investors. However, in some cases limitations on voting rights and on the amount of dividends payable might reduce the attractiveness of investing to non-patrons.

3. Control and the Decision-Making Process

For smaller businesses in particular, if the cooperative form is used, management must spend a fair amount of time engaging in member relations, since the members have substantial control over the business and are also its primary (and sometimes only) customers. For that matter, in the early period of the cooperative's formation, during the time before management is engaged, the founders of the cooperative will have to work together with other members to form policies and make key decisions. Because of the one-member/one-vote principle of the cooperative, the cooperative's manager and board will have to expend more effort for obtaining support for key initiatives than would the CEO and board of directors of a corporation or the management of an LLC. A necessary step such as drafting and adopting bylaws will require cooperation and approval by the cooperative's members, whereas in the small corporation such a step is usually taken care of in short order by the initial shareholders. The cooperative form thus might not be suitable for a new enterprise that requires centralized management or rapid decisions by management.

4. Conclusion

The previous discussion indicates that the traditional cooperative form is certainly not appropriate for every kind of business enterprise. Whether to use the cooperative form for a particular business enterprise appears to be driven by a few basic questions that focus on the unique structure of the cooperative form of business:

- Do the founders of the enterprise intend for the economic benefits of the enterprise to go to the owners of the enterprise, rather than outside investors?
- Do the founders intend for the enterprise to provide a specific product or service?
- Are the founders willing for all of the customers obtaining the goods or services from the enterprise to also own the enterprise?
- Are the founders willing for the enterprise to be governed on a democratic basis by the owner/customers, that is, on a one-member/one-vote basis?

If the answers to these questions are "yes," then the cooperative form might well be worth considering when deciding on the appropriate structure for the business enterprise.

C. Formation of Cooperatives

Organizing a cooperative typically requires formation under the applicable state statute. In some cases, the state has a statutory scheme directly applicable to the cooperative, such as with agricultural cooperatives or electrical cooperatives. In other cases, multiple statutes may apply, or no statutes that apply. In all cases where a statute governs incorporation or formation, however, the statute provides the specific requirements that the founders must meet to achieve incorporation or formation. Although it is of course possible to operate as a cooperative without organizing the cooperative under a statute, doing so results in the personal liability of the group's members for the obligations of the cooperative and could also create tax and governance difficulties for the group's members.

For corporations, LLCs, and limited partnerships, determining which state statute controls formation of the entity is usually easy. Typically, each state has one statutory scheme for each type of entity, and the requirements (and necessary forms) are made available by the secretary of state or similar authority. Because of the development of model acts, such as the Uniform Limited Partnership Act, and their adoption by most states, the requirements for formation are often similar from one state to another.

Not so for cooperatives. Because in many states cooperative statutes were developed in response to specific types of cooperatives becoming widely used, or in reaction to political events or theories concerning the proper form and function of cooperatives, in any given state various statutes might exist that are applicable to particular kinds of cooperatives. As a result, state statutes governing the organization of cooperatives vary widely in their requirements. These varying statutory schemes mean that for any given state, typically there is no general statute for the formation of a cooperative, as there is for corporations, LLCs, and limited partnerships. Some states, such as Nevada, Wisconsin, and Oregon, however, have cooperative statutes that allow incorporation of a cooperative for any lawful purpose (with limited exceptions) and, thus, allow cooperatives to be formed for any type of business enterprise.

Another peculiarity resulting from the way in which cooperative statutes have evolved is that in many states cooperatives can be formed as either stock or non-stock organizations. In some states, however, the ability to form a stock cooperative is limited to certain lines of business, such as agriculture. Stock cooperatives, as the name implies, issue common stock and, in some cases, preferred stock, with ownership of common stock carrying with it voting rights in the cooperative. In the nonstock cooperative, the cooperative issues membership certificates that include voting rights and membership in the cooperative, and capital certificates that are similar to the preferred stock issued by stock cooperatives. While either the stock or non-stock structure maybe suitable, founders less acquainted with cooperatives might find it easier to understand the stock structure because of its similarity to the structure used by corporations.

In the event that none of the available cooperative statutes is suitable for formation of the proposed cooperative enterprise, the business could be incorporated under the state's general incorporation statute or non-profit code or formed under the state's LLC act. If this course is taken, the bylaws or operating agreement must be written in such a way as to provide for operation of the entity as a cooperative. In addition, the entity's financial operations will have to be structured to resemble those of a cooperative as closely as possible.

Once the decision to form a cooperative is made and the appropriate state statute is selected, the articles must be drafted and filed. In most cases, the statute will provide for incorporation of the cooperative, and the articles of incorporation will be similar to those of a corporation, although the statute governing formation must be consulted concerning any special requirements. Typically the articles will contain the name of the cooperative, its principal place of business, the names of the incorporators, and information about the cooperative's capital structure. If the cooperative is a stock cooperative, the articles might also specify the classes of stock (e.g., common and preferred) and the number of authorized shares of stock. Just as with a corporation, once the articles are filed with the appropriate authority, the life of the cooperative begins.

Some modern statutes now provide for the organization of cooperatives that share characteristics of unincorporated entities such as LLCs. Under these statutes, articles of organization similar to those of an LLC will be filed. As with incorporated cooperatives, the statute governing formation will determine whether any special requirements apply. Typically, the articles of organization, like the articles of incorporation of the incorporated cooperative, will contain the name of the cooperative, its principal place of business, and the names of the incorporators.

The bylaws are the next document typically prepared for the cooperative. (Even those statutes that provide for organization of unincorporated cooperatives typically allow for bylaws, rather than an operating agreement.) In contrast to the cooperative's articles, which are similar in many respects to the articles of incorporation of corporations, the cooperative's bylaws are often very different in substance from their corporate counterparts. This is caused in part by the need to conform the bylaws to the enabling statute used for creation of the cooperative. Another cause is the unique structure of the cooperative itself, and the need to include provisions that address the special relationship between the cooperative and its members. The financial structure of cooperatives also requires specialized provisions that address patronage refunds.

Aside from these legal considerations, though, is the practical requirement of addressing the potential (and often actual) conflicts that arise between the cooperative's board of directors and its members, and, in the case of federated cooperatives, the conflicts that arise not only between the federated cooperative and its member cooperatives, but among the member cooperatives themselves and their boards. (See Chapter IV for more information on federated cooperatives, which are owned by other cooperatives and provide goods and services to their member cooperatives.) For all of these reasons, the cooperative's bylaws are often much more detailed than the typical bylaws of the corporation or the operating agreement of the LLC.

Another consideration in drafting the cooperative's bylaws concerns the use of form bylaws. When drafting the governance documents of corporations and LLCs, form documents are often useful in providing the initial structure and certain standard basic provisions. Because many of the laws applicable to corporations and LLCs are very similar from state to state, standard provisions in bylaws or an operating agreement used in one state might very well prove useful in others as well. With the cooperative, however, the statutes governing the operation and formation of cooperatives vary not only from state to state, but within each state depending on the type of cooperative being formed. For this reason, while a form set of bylaws might be of some use, it will likely be necessary to draft custom bylaws. In doing so, it is essential to dissect the state statutory scheme (and any relevant federal tax laws) applicable to the cooperative and make sure that every element of the bylaws is in compliance with the applicable laws.

A sizeable portion of the cooperative's bylaws will be devoted to governance matters involving the cooperative's members. The bylaws will include requirements for membership, procedures for annual and special meetings of the members, and procedures for elections of directors by the members. Although provisions concerning the members might seem similar to the provisions in corporate bylaws that address shareholders, critical differences arise from the one-member/one-vote principle of the cooperative structure and from the fact that the members are all customers of the cooperative. As to the first point, the bylaws must address, from both a legal and a practical perspective, the decisions that will require the consent of the members as opposed to, or in some cases in addition to, the approval of the board. Especially in larger cooperatives, where the members are other cooperatives, care must be taken in allocating decision-making power and defining voting requirements, not only to enable reasonable speed and efficiency in decision making, but also to prevent "gaming" of the bylaws by the cooperative's members.

The fact that the cooperative's members are also its customers leads to further possible complexities in drafting the bylaws. It is important to recognize that in the case of a cooperative, its customers are not only its focus, but are the sole reason for its formation and existence. The purpose for which the cooperative was formed was to provide goods or services to the original customers who established the entity and to provide those goods or services in the manner desired by the customers (e.g., at the lowest possible cost, or in accordance with the members' quality requirements). This focus on the customers, most, if not all, of whom are also members, requires distinctive provisions in the bylaws not only concerning financial aspects of the cooperative/member relationship, but careful attention to the governance provisions as well. Also, in larger cooperatives with members scattered across a large geographic region, special provisions might be required that divide the cooperative's territory into districts and that allow members in each district to elect one or more directors. Members/customers in different regions may well have differing expectations or requirements of the cooperative and district representation may help in resolving these differences.

Although we have touched on the basic legal requirements for starting a cooperative, many other steps involved are beyond the scope of this book. For example, the cooperative will likely need to select a manager or CEO, have a membership drive, consider and evaluate sources of capital, and select financial and legal advisers, among other things. As with any business endeavor, the success of the cooperative will depend to a great degree on the skill and enthusiasm of its leaders. To a greater degree than other entities, however, the cooperative's success also depends on the strength of the relationships among the cooperative's leaders and its members/customers. Drafting instruments that set forth fair, easily understandable rules governing the roles, rights and responsibilities of the cooperative's participants will go a long way toward ensuring that such relationships remain healthy and that the cooperative is a success.

IV

Types of Cooperatives and Cooperative Structure

The purpose of this chapter is to discuss the different ways in which cooperatives may be categorized. This is not just an academic exercise, since the state laws and federal tax laws applicable to cooperatives are usually geared toward cooperatives in specific business categories rather than the cooperative structure in general. Also, understanding the traditional categories of cooperatives is a further step toward achieving the "general knowledge" of cooperatives that is essential in negotiating with cooperatives or in representing clients that are cooperatives.

Because the primary purpose of the cooperative is to provide benefits for its members, it is logical that cooperatives can be categorized on the basis of what they accomplish for their members. For example, service cooperatives provide services to their members, such as telecommunications, financial services, and housing. Within these general categories, cooperatives can be further categorized by business sector. Because the typical cooperative is organized for a single purpose, such as providing insurance services or providing electric power, a particular cooperative will usually fit within a specific category, unlike corporations, which typically provide a wide mix of various goods and services.

Another method of classifying cooperatives is perhaps less obvious to those with limited exposure to the cooperative structure. Because a cooperative's members can be individuals, other cooperatives, or other types of business entities, cooperatives can be classified on the basis of their membership structure. It is perhaps intuitive that a cooperative made up of other cooperatives, rather than individuals, would face additional challenges as to operation and governance, and for this and other reasons it is important to have a general understanding of the ways in which cooperatives can be structured.

A. Classification by Business Purpose

Typically, it is easier to classify a given cooperative by its business purpose than it is to classify another type of business entity by business purpose, especially where larger businesses are concerned. Classifying corporations or limited liability companies (LLCs) by their business purpose can be difficult, since many companies are diversified and have more than one business focus. Because the focus of the typical for-profit company is on achieving maximum profits for its owners, it makes at least theoretical sense for the company to enter into any legitimate line of business that can generate profits. Although there are practical limitations on smaller companies in this regard, since entering into multiple lines of business might be limited by capital requirements and by the available expertise of the owners and managers, larger companies can hire the needed expertise required to enter into multiple potentially profitable markets.

1. Restrictions on Lines of Business

Although corporations might own and operate several lines of business, and large conglomerates might operate dozens, the typical cooperative conducts business on the basis of a single product or service, such as, for example, providing electricity to members or providing financial services for other cooperatives. While the limitation of the cooperative to a single purpose is driven in part by state and federal law, this limitation is also a natural result of the way in which cooperatives are formed. Typically, producers or consumers with a common interest form a cooperative to obtain benefits related to that common interest. The members thus do not form the cooperative with a general motive, such as obtaining profits or providing general services, but through an interest in obtaining or providing a specific product or service. The primary interest of the members, and thus the cooperative, is in achieving success in providing the product or service demanded.

The state laws applicable to cooperatives have also played a part in ensuring that the typical cooperative restricts itself to one line of business. State statutes addressing cooperatives were usually enacted reactively, rather than proactively, and are often intended to cover a specific type of cooperative, such as the agricultural cooperative or the electric cooperative. These statutes often restrict the cooperatives formed under them to conducting business directly related to their primary purposes. For example, in Florida and Illinois, agricultural cooperatives are formed under statutes devoted specifically to agricultural cooperative marketing associations, with the allowed purposes of the cooperative specified by statute.[1] A New York state statute providing for the formation of cooperative corporations specifies various purposes for which such cooperatives can be formed, including agricultural cooperatives, housing cooperatives, and worker cooperatives.[2]

Cooperatives formed under such statutes must carefully consider whether it is advisable to enter into new lines of business, since such a move could lead to legal challenges from other businesses within the industry or from the state in which the cooperative is organized. A cooperative that has invested substantial capital in a new line of business could find itself forced to divest the business at a loss. Such a result could even lead to actions against the cooperative and its officers and directors by the members. For example, the Supreme Court of Kentucky recently held that because an electric cooperative was limited by statute to providing services related to electric power, it could not provide propane gas or other nonelectric services to its customers.[3] In some cases cooperatives can successfully argue that a new line of business falls within the permissible purposes enumerated in the statute; for example, the Supreme Court of Montana held that a telephone cooperative could offer dial-up Internet services, since such services were sufficiently similar to telephone service to be allowable under the applicable statute.[4]

Some states, including Alaska, Colorado, Iowa, and Minnesota, have statutes allowing the formation of cooperatives for the transaction of any lawful business (subject to certain exceptions, such as the ability to perform insurance or banking functions).[5] Under such statutory schemes, actions against cooperatives entering into different lines of business are less likely to succeed, even where cooperatives are subject to other restrictions applicable to their particular line of business. For example, the Colorado Court of Appeals held that an electric cooperative could invest in for-profit nonelectric subsidiaries, since the state enabling statute for electric cooperatives incorporated by reference a general cooperative statute that allowed the formation of cooperatives for the transaction of any lawful business.[6] As can be seen, the ability of cooperatives to enter into different lines of business depends to a great extent on the wording of the state statutes applicable to the particular cooperative.

Sometimes state statutes go so far as to specify lines of business that cooperatives cannot enter. For example, electric cooperatives in some states are specifically restricted from offering services related to cable television, natural gas, or propane gas.[7] These restrictions are usually of newer vintage, and result from the lobbying efforts of businesses and industries that fear the competitive impact of cooperatives entering into the line of business in question. In some cases, industry groups obtain restrictive legislation on the basis of arguments that cooperatives can obtain unfair advantages over other types of business entities because of government-backed financing programs and other special programs developed for cooperatives. However, in some states, cooperatives have successfully lobbied for legislation specifically authorizing cooperatives to enter into certain lines of business. For example, in Georgia, electric cooperatives obtained the ability, subject to certain restrictions, to enter into the retail natural gas market through gas marketing affiliates.[8]

Although noncooperative businesses often cite a number of reasons why cooperatives should be restricted from moving into their industry, the main concern of noncooperative businesses is a direct result of the cooperative's unique structure. Because the cooperative's members/customers are also its owners, they have multiple reasons for remaining loyal not only to the cooperative's products and services, but also to the cooperative itself. In addition, because of the principle of democratic control, the cooperative's members/customers each have a similar sense of control over the cooperative's course. For these reasons, if the cooperative offers a new product or service, the cooperative's members are likely to take it, even if doing so requires them to switch from their current provider. Further, cooperatives are often seen as the "local company" with a close identification with consumers and the local community, thus having a marketing advantage over competitors. Also, cooperatives also have an effect on local prices for products, supplies, and services, and cooperative pricing sometimes results in adjustments in pricing by their competitors. It is this power of the cooperative, fueled by the loyalty of its members, that sometimes leads to concerted efforts by industry groups to keep cooperatives from expanding their lines of business and entering into new industries.

While, as we have noted, the typical cooperative focuses on one line of business, over time cooperatives often expand into additional lines of business. Any such expansion is usually gradual and taken with great precaution. If a cooperative is successful in its chosen line of business, its members might well seek to have the cooperative offer them related products or services. In some cases, the cooperative's management might envision using the initial product or service as a springboard to offering a package of related products and services.

If statutory restrictions are not an issue, such expansion can be a great benefit to the cooperative and its members. For example, some electric cooperatives now offer home security services, Internet services, and natural gas services. Some agricultural cooperatives that sold commodities for their members have diversified into processing such commodities and selling branded goods to wholesalers and consumers. In cases where this type of expansion requires resources that typically cannot be provided by the traditional cooperative, such as capital infusions from outside investors, cooperatives can now explore the use of forms such as the new generation cooperative or limited cooperative association that maintain the cooperative principles while offering some of the attributes of LLCs. (See Chapter II for further information on new generation cooperatives and limited cooperative associations.)

2. Categories of Cooperatives by Business Purpose

Now that we have explored the reasons why it is easier to categorize cooperatives according to business purpose, let us turn to the categories themselves. Cooperatives can be placed into one of five broad categories related to business purpose:

- Consumer cooperatives that provide retail goods to their members.
- Service cooperatives that provide services to their members.
- Producer/marketing cooperatives that market goods for their members.
- Purchasing cooperatives that purchase supplies for their members to enable the members to produce goods or perform services.
- Worker cooperatives that provide a workplace for members and provide goods and services to nonmembers.

Although a variety of labels have been applied to these categories over the years, the basic categories listed above have remained the same.

Consumer cooperatives. The consumer cooperative acts on behalf of its members to purchase goods at wholesale and to sell these goods to its members. Some of the earliest consumer cooperatives included grocery stores that provided groceries to members at affordable prices. Other consumer cooperatives provide hardware, household appliances, and lawn and garden equipment. Almost any item that a consumer might require can be provided by a consumer cooperative. For example, many natural food stores in the United States are cooperative in structure, with one of the largest examples being the Puget Consumers Co-op in the Puget Sound Region, which operates eight stores and has 40,000 members. Recent statistics indicate that the total revenues of wholesale and retail cooperative grocery stores alone are over $33 billion.[9]

More so than other kinds of cooperatives, consumer cooperatives often provide goods to nonmembers. Nonmembers typically pay higher prices than members, however, and members may enjoy other benefits arising from membership in the cooperative. In some cases, members work in the cooperative's retail locations and earn discounts or pay membership fees based on their work.

Consumer cooperatives in the same line of business sometimes band together and form wholesale cooperatives that purchase goods from producers and manufacturers and provide such goods at wholesale to the member consumer cooperatives. In this way, the individual members can obtain additional cost savings and the consumer cooperatives can leverage their bargaining power when making purchases in the wholesale marketplace.

Service cooperatives. As the name implies, service cooperatives provide a specific service to their members, such as financial services, housing, health care, insurance, child care, cleaning services, electricity, and funeral arrangements. Perhaps a more accurate name for these cooperatives would be retail service cooperatives, since there are other cooperatives (discussed in more detail in the following) that provide services to other cooperatives.

Many service cooperatives were formed on the basis of a specific need. For example, in cities with a high cost of living it might be necessary to form a cooperative to provide housing or child care services, since otherwise such services would be unavailable or prohibitively expensive. In rural areas, particular kinds of service cooperatives might be formed because other businesses did not find it cost effective to offer such services in the communities involved. For instance, telephone and electric cooperatives were formed, with the assistance of the government, to offer these services in areas in which such services would otherwise be unavailable. And of course credit unions provided financial services to many who had been unable to obtain services from traditional banks.

Service cooperatives provide a good example of the intangible benefits that accrue to the cooperative's members/customers because of the unique structure of the cooperative. Because a customer coming in the door to obtain services is usually an owner of the cooperative, in many cases the customer enjoys a more personal level of service than would be obtained from a similar, noncooperative business. Also, in many cases, the person providing service is a member and owner of the cooperative as well. For example, the member obtaining a loan from a credit union will interact with employees who are also members and owners of the institution. On a smaller scale, in a child care cooperative, typically the caregiver and the person obtaining child care are both members and owners of the cooperative. It is not surprising that such a relationship between the company and the customer could result both in an intangible pride of ownership and control and in a more satisfying transactional experience.

While the retail service cooperative provides services on the retail level to its members, the wholesale service cooperative provides services to other cooperatives. For example, in a given industry, a cooperative might be formed by retail cooperatives to offer accounting and back-office services to its member cooperatives. For example, Southeastern Data Cooperative provides billing and accounting services to electric cooperatives and municipal utilities across the country.[10] A cooperative might also be formed to provide insurance services for member cooperatives. Cooperative banks such as the federally chartered National Cooperative Bank provide financing to a wide variety of cooperatives. Retail cooperatives have a strong incentive to encourage the growth of their wholesale cooperative, since obtaining additional members results in more leverage for the wholesale cooperative and better pricing for its members. Depending on the industry and applicable law, the wholesale cooperative might also be able to achieve growth by providing services to nonmembers.

Producer/marketing cooperatives. Producer cooperatives, often referred to as marketing cooperatives, sell the products of their members into the relevant market. Because this category includes agricultural cooperatives, this type of cooperative is perhaps the most familiar to the general public. Considering only agricultural cooperatives for the moment, producer cooperatives market virtually every kind of agricultural product, including dairy products, fruits and vegetables, sugar, livestock, and grains. When agricultural cooperatives first came into widespread use in the late nineteenth and early twentieth century, most members were small farmers, and the cooperative structure allowed such farmers to leverage their bargaining power with purchasers and achieve higher prices and better terms. These cooperatives also allowed their members to control the processing and marketing of their products as well, and early cooperatives owned and operated cotton gins, grain elevators, milk plants, and various other ventures designed to help members obtain cost-effective means of producing market-ready products.

As our agricultural markets have changed, agricultural cooperatives have changed as well. One significant change of fairly recent vintage is the progression toward vertical integration. The new generation cooperatives discussed in Chapter II have purchased factories and processing equipment to control the path of agricultural commodities from the field to the consumer's table. In some cases, vertical integration includes packaging and branding food products for sale to wholesale companies, while in other cases cooperatives even obtain shelf space in grocery store chains and market their branded products directly to consumers.

Although some agricultural cooperatives have achieved this type of vertical integration, many have formed regional cooperatives that perform some or all of the tasks involved in processing and marketing agricultural goods. In this scenario, the agricultural producer cooperative focuses on the sale of raw farm products, and one or more regional cooperatives in which the producer cooperative is a member provides processing, packaging, distribution, and marketing services. In essence, the regional cooperatives are service cooperatives that provide services to their producer cooperative members. Some regional cooperatives of this type, such as Land O'Lakes, have been in existence for quite some time and have built up highly recognizable brand names under which their members' products are sold. Other well-established brand names developed by cooperatives for their members' products include Ocean Spray, SunKist, Sun-Maid, Sunsweet, Tree Top, and Welch's.

Although many producer cooperatives are agricultural cooperatives, other types of products are marketed by cooperatives as well. Producer cooperatives have been particularly effective in achieving greater visibility for the handicrafts and artwork created by local artisans and artists. In many cases, the cooperative rents or purchases retail space to showcase the products of its members or promotes products on the Internet or through other advertising channels. Although the individual artist would not have the resources to publicize his or her work or to obtain "shelf space" in a gallery or shop, the cooperative can achieve these goals as well as providing an opportunity for shoppers to access a variety of works in a single location. For example, Quayside Art Gallery in Pensacola, Florida has over

200 artists as members, who also volunteer as staff members of the gallery.[11] The U.S. Department of Agriculture and some states have provided educational and financial assistance for the formation of craft cooperatives in rural communities.[12]

Purchasing cooperatives. Purchasing cooperatives are typically formed by other companies, including but not limited to cooperatives, and provide their members with the goods and supplies necessary to conduct their businesses. Although the general public is perhaps least familiar with purchasing cooperatives, these cooperatives represent an important part of the economy and, in fact, are a critical link in the procurement chain that allows small businesses to compete effectively with larger business enterprises. Through the combined buying power of its members, the purchasing cooperative has the means to obtain goods and supplies in bulk at competitive prices and thus enable its members to enjoy success in a marketplace filled with larger competitors.

One type of purchasing cooperative provides its members with the supplies and equipment necessary to produce their products and provide their services. For example, agricultural purchasing cooperatives are well established, and provide farmers with required equipment and supplies, including farm equipment, building supplies, feed, seed, fuel, propane, and crop protection products. As another example, the Educational & Institutional Cooperative purchases health care and educational supplies for its members, which include over 1500 universities, colleges, and hospitals.[13] Fast food restaurant owners have also formed purchasing cooperatives that provide them with food, equipment, supplies, and other items necessary for their operations. The Unified Foodservice Purchasing Co-op performs this function for all corporate and many franchise-owned KFC, Long John Silver's, Pizza Hut, and Taco Bell restaurants.[14] Thousands of other, lesser-known purchasing cooperatives provide procurement services for business owners across the country.

Purchasing cooperatives in other industries actually provide their members with the products that they sell to the public. For example, Ace Hardware is a purchasing cooperative wholly owned by independent hardware stores, and provides its member stores with products similar to those sold by other hardware chains.[15] While an individual dealer procuring products on its own would have difficulty in achieving prices competitive with chain hardware stores, through the purchasing cooperative, store owners are able to level the playing field. Purchasing cooperatives formed by grocery stores are another example of this type of purchasing cooperative. Independent grocers that obtain their goods from purchasing cooperatives can more easily compete with larger grocery chain stores.

Worker cooperatives. Worker cooperatives are businesses collectively owned by the workers who operate the business. Unlike other cooperatives, such as service cooperatives, worker cooperatives often sell most of their goods or services to nonmembers. The function of the members is to own, operate and manage the business enterprise. For example, some restaurants and bakeries are worker-owned cooperatives in which the workers perform all required work for the business and collectively manage the business. Also, some organic grocery stores are worker cooperatives. National organizations such as the U.S. Federation of Worker Cooperatives provide assistance to and publicity for such worker cooperatives.

There is little legislation in the United States aimed at worker cooperatives, and as a result most worker cooperatives organize under their state's general cooperative statute, if one exists, or organize under their state's corporation statutes. While worker cooperatives are relatively rare in the United States, such cooperatives are quite popular in Europe. The Mondragon Cooperative Corporation, located in Spain, is referred to as the largest worker cooperative in the world, and now consists of over 250 companies with over 80,000 worker/owners.

B. Classification by Structure

In addition to being classified by business purpose, cooperatives can also be classified by their membership structure. The most familiar type of cooperative is one in which the members are the end users of the cooperative's products or services or are the producers of the products or services sold by the cooperative on their behalf. This type of cooperative is sometimes called a centralized or local cooperative. In contrast, the federated cooperative is owned by centralized cooperatives, and provides goods and services to its member cooperatives that ultimately are provided to the individual members of the member cooperatives. Another type of cooperative is the so-called mixed or hybrid cooperative, in which the members are both cooperatives and end users.

When agricultural marketing cooperatives were first formed, centralized cooperatives tended to be cooperatives that served local communities, while federated cooperatives were organized to serve larger geographic areas. Centralized cooperatives had limited functions such as assembling products for sale or providing commodity grading services, while the federated cooperative might perform more complex or sophisticated services, such as negotiating with buyers for products or manufacturing products into finished form. Over time, advances in transportation and technology allowed centralized cooperatives to expand their geographic reach to the point that centralized cooperatives today can and often do own and operate vertically integrated enterprises that turn raw products into finished merchandise. In an attempt to differentiate between the various sizes of centralized cooperatives, which might range in size from small, locally owned enterprises to large operations that span several states, some refer to the smaller cooperatives as "local cooperatives." For our purposes, however, distinguishing between centralized and federated cooperatives is sufficient.

How do the members decide which type of structure to use for their cooperative? In some cases cooperatives might decide to form a federated cooperative to negotiate for goods and services on the wholesale level and to provide focused, region- or nationwide branding and advertising. In other cases the cooperative's industry, combined with market forces, might make the formation of a federated cooperative necessary. For example, groups of centralized electric cooperatives found that joining together and forming federated cooperatives to build power plants and procure power for them in the wholesale markets provided them with increased negotiating strength and lower prices for their consumers. At times cooperatives have found it easier to form a federated cooperative to provide specific services for them, such as accounting services, since a federated cooperative will have a better understanding of cooperatives and their unique needs.

In some cases, what might at first glance appear to be a federated cooperative is actually a centralized cooperative. Confusion is most likely to occur where the cooperative is made up of other companies, rather than individuals. For example, even though Ace Hardware serves members across the country, it is structured as a centralized cooperative, since its members, the individual hardware stores that obtain goods from Ace, are not themselves cooperatives. On the other hand, where cooperative grocery stores join together to form a supply cooperative, the supply cooperative would be a federated cooperative, since the grocery stores are themselves cooperatives.[16] With these examples, the end result is largely the same, since in both cases small businesses are joining forces with other, similar businesses in order to achieve greater market penetration and increase the ability to compete with larger chains.

Let us now turn to a more detailed examination of the cooperative structures already discussed.

1. Centralized Cooperatives

The centralized cooperative is owned and controlled directly by members that are also its end users. Its members might be individuals or businesses. Like a corporation, the centralized cooperative has a primary office, a board of directors, and a manager or CEO. "Centralized" is not necessarily equivalent to small, and in fact the centralized cooperative might have multiple divisions, districts, manufacturing plants, or retail outlets, depending on the type of cooperative. To run its operations the centralized cooperative might have numerous branch offices headed by managers that report to the central office.

A good example of a larger centralized cooperative is Blue Diamond Growers, a cooperative made up of about 3000 almond growers.[17] The cooperative initially helped its members obtain better prices for their crops and helped members add value by creating a brand name to advertise and sell what had been a commodity product. The cooperative now markets its members' products worldwide. The cooperative elects a nine-member board of directors, with each director elected from the members residing in a directorial district. The cooperative is managed by a President/CEO (chief executive officer) and a CFO (chief financial officer). Although Blue Diamond has operations across the country and offices worldwide, it maintains a centralized structure in which its members elect a single board of directors.

2. Federated Cooperatives

A federated cooperative is simply a cooperative owned by other cooperatives. The other cooperatives are represented on the board of directors of the federated cooperative's board. Smaller federated cooperatives might have representatives from each member cooperative on the federated cooperative's board, while larger federated cooperatives might have member cooperatives assigned to districts, with representatives on the board from each district. For example, Oglethorpe Power Corporation, a federated power cooperative located in Georgia, is managed by a board of directors elected by its members, which are centralized power cooperatives serving members/customers throughout the state. The territory covered by the members is divided into districts, with certain seats on the board assigned to each district.

Depending on what the state cooperative law allows, voting rights for the members of a federated cooperative might be assigned on a one-member/one-vote basis, or through a variety of other means, including voting rights that correlate to patronage, member size, or other factors. Like the centralized cooperative, the federated cooperative typically has a board of directors and a manager. However, the federated cooperative's cooperative members also have boards of directors and managers, with managers and members of the member cooperatives often serving on the board of the federated cooperative. As one might imagine, conflict-of-interest issues can arise when a federated cooperative's board is required to vote on matters that affect the cooperative members, especially where board members represent or work for those cooperative members.

3. Hybrid or Mixed Cooperatives

Hybrid cooperatives, also referred at times as mixed cooperatives, have characteristics of both federated and centralized cooperatives. Hybrid cooperatives include in their membership both cooperatives and individual members. Under this structure, cooperatives and individual members vote for the members of the hybrid cooperative's board of directors. A good example of a hybrid cooperative is Land O'Lakes, a national food and agricultural cooperative whose members include individual dairy producers as well as over one thousand local cooperatives.[18] Land O'Lakes is a producer cooperative that sells its members' dairy products across the country, as well as a purchasing cooperative that sells products such as feed and seed to its cooperative members. Individual producers thus might be direct members of the hybrid cooperative, or indirect members through their status as members of a local cooperative that is a member of the hybrid cooperative.

Notes

1. Fla. Stat. Ann. § 618.06; 805 Ill. Comp. Stat. 315/4.
2. N.Y. Coop. Corp. Law Art. 2, § 13.
3. Lewis v. Jackson Energy Co-op Corp., 189 S.W.2d 87 (Ky. 2005).
4. Weber v. Interbel Tel. Co-op, Inc., 80 P.3d 88 (Mont. 2003).
5. Alaska Stat. § 10.15.005; Colo. Rev. Stat. Ann. § 7-55-102; Iowa Code Ann. § 501A.501; Mich. Comp. Laws. Ann. § 308A.101.
6. Bontrager v. La Plata Elec. Ass'n Inc., 68 P.3d 555 (Colo. App. 2003).
7. O.C.G.A. § 46-3-178 (electric cooperative prohibited from operating cable television system).
8. O.C.G.A. § 46-4-164.
9. *Cooperative Businesses in the United States, A 2005 Snapshot*, NATIONAL COOPERATIVE MONTH, *available at* http://www.coopmonth.coop/download_files/economicimpact.final.pdf.
10. http://www.sedata.com/corporate.
11. http://www.quaysidegallery.com.
12. The USDA has published a directory of American arts and crafts cooperatives, although the directory was last updated in 1996. See http://www.rurdev.usda.gov/rbs/pub/sr40.pdf. A more recent directory can be found at http://people.hofstra.edu/faculty/Martha_J_Kreisel/directory_of_craft_cooperatives.html.
13. http://www.eandi.org.
14. http://www.ufpc.com.
15. Ace Hardware Business Opportunities, http://www.myace.com.
16. Of course, a cooperative might have both cooperative and no-cooperative members.
17. Blue Diamond Growers, http://www.bluediamond.com.
18. Land O'Lakes, http://www.landolakes.com.

Further Reading

Cooperative Organization and Structure, Farmer Cooperatives in the United States, USDA COOPERATIVE INFORMATION REPORT No. 1, Section 6 (1988).
Co-ops 101: An Introduction to Cooperatives, USDA COOPERATIVE INFORMATION REPORT No. 55 (1997).
KIMBERLY A. ZEULI and ROBERT CROPP, COOPERATIVES: PRINCIPLES AND PRACTICES IN THE 21ST CENTURY, (4th ed. 2004).

V

Operation and Governance

At first glance, the operation and governance of the cooperative appear similar to that of any typical corporation. The cooperative has members that are in many respects much like shareholders. Cooperatives are generally governed by a board of directors and have officers with duties and obligations similar to those of officers in corporations. However, even those aspects of operation and governance that appear to be taken directly from corporate models must be understood in light of cooperative principles and values. Upon closer examination, the operation and governance of cooperatives present a variety of issues that result directly from the unique structure of the cooperative and the nature of the relationship between the cooperative and its members. In this chapter, we will explore both the similarities and the differences in operation and governance of cooperatives and other business entities.

In examining cooperative operation and governance, it is important to keep in mind that the features of today's "traditional" cooperatives are the result of a long and fruitful period of experimentation and development and that cooperatives, like other business organizations, vary greatly in size, purpose, and sophistication. While we have attempted to draw conclusions in this chapter about operation and governance principles of cooperatives in general, the cooperative form permits a wide variety of governance models, and this chapter does not pretend to address all of them.

A. Members

While a typical corporation has shareholders, the cooperative has members, with each member's ownership represented by shares in the cooperative or a membership certificate. As has been repeatedly alluded to in this book, the unique relationship between cooperatives and their members, which features the important principle of democratic member control, is a hallmark of the cooperative entity. How do we define a member? What is unique about the member's relationship with the cooperative? How is a member similar to or different from a shareholder? What powers do members typically have related to the operation and governance of the cooperative? The answers to these questions will provide insight into the member's role in cooperative operations and governance.

1. Members and Their Relationship with the Cooperative

While there are clear differences between members of a cooperative and corporate shareholders, a brief comparison of the two can help illustrate important features of the members' relationship with their cooperative. In many respects, the member and the shareholder are much alike.

Members of a cooperative, like corporate shareholders, have an ownership interest in the entity and elect the entity's board of directors. Members of a cooperative have voting rights very similar to those of shareholders and have the same limited liability as shareholders for debts and liabilities of the entity. It is often the case that members, like shareholders, have specific approval rights regarding certain actions of the entity. For example, under many cooperative statutes, membership votes are required for approval of mergers and acquisitions. Finally, members are often afforded control rights similar to those of a corporate shareholder, such as the ability to bring derivative actions.

The member/cooperative relationship is unique, however, in at least four respects. First, as discussed in Chapter VI, while a cooperative member is entitled to capital credits (patronage refunds) when cooperative revenues exceed costs, the member's objective is not economic return. Instead, ownership is focused on the acquisition of the service or good provided by the cooperative. Second, while a member typically has some limited right to transfer his or her membership, the membership interest, unlike a share of stock, is not intended as a transferable, saleable investment with the purpose of generating gain for the member. Third, while shareholders have weighted control based on the number of shares held, in the typical cooperative each member has one vote irrespective of the volume of business done with the cooperative. For example, in an electric cooperative, a small residential consumer has the same voting strength as a large industrial customer. Finally, unlike a shareholder who can be an owner without being a consumer of the corporation's products and services, one cannot be an owner of a cooperative without also being a consumer of the cooperative's products or services.

The last point is an important distinction between the cooperative and the corporation. Members are by definition customers of the cooperative. By virtue of that linkage, a cooperative member/customer has a degree of control over the quality and price of the cooperative's products and services not enjoyed by the typical customer of a corporation, whose main point of control consists of the ability to choose whether or not to deal with the corporation. It is because of this linkage between the member and customer relationships that the customer benefits economically in the form of capital credits (patronage refunds) when the cooperative's revenues exceed its costs.

2. Governance Powers of Members

While, as discussed later in this chapter, the business and affairs of a cooperative are typically under the direction of the board of directors, the ultimate responsibility of cooperative governance lies with the cooperative's members. Members typically exercise their authority by voting on a one-member/one-vote basis. The exercise of the members' authority is easy to see in a smaller cooperative, where many of the members may actively participate in the operation and governance of the cooperative. Yet even in a larger cooperative the membership as a whole has the ability and responsibility to participate in the governance of the cooperative.

Most states secure the rights of member participation by specific statutory provisions which address, for example, periodic annual meetings of members, the rights of members to participate in the election of directors, the rights of members to certain specific internal corporate information and records, the rights of members to approve certain major corporate actions such as the sale of all or substantially all of the assets of cooperative or a merger, and a right to bring derivative actions.

In addition to these powers, most state statutes require member approval of the articles of incorporation, the bylaws, and any amendments to those documents. The bylaws can impose additional requirements for approval; for example, the bylaws could require that the affirmative vote of three-quarters of the members is required to amend the bylaws. Because of the importance of the bylaws to the governance of the cooperative, this power of the members is of critical importance. For example, subject to any restrictions under applicable state law, the members can amend the bylaws to change the composition of the board of directors or to expand or diminish the number of officers of the cooperative.

While the members have the power to make themselves heard at any point in time, in practice, the members as a body exercise much of their decision-making authority at the annual meeting of members. At the annual meeting, the members elect directors, hear management's report on the cooperative's operations, and have a forum to make themselves heard. In addition, the bylaws often provide a method for the members to compel the board to call for a special meeting of the members upon proper notice.

On the basis of the foregoing, the practitioner who works with typical business organizations might conclude that a member of a cooperative is really no different than a shareholder of a corporation. It can be difficult to articulate what it is that makes the member-cooperative relationship unique, and reading that members control their cooperative may not impress the reader as a significant difference from the control rights of shareholders. However, based on our experience in working with cooperatives, the principle of democratic control is a significant element in making the member-cooperative relationship unique.

In all but the smallest corporations, shareholders have the ability to control the corporation, but normally few have an incentive to do so. Shareholders might or might not purchase the products or services sold by the corporation, and typically do not have a close relationship with the corporation or with each other. The shareholders' primary interest in the corporation is an economic one. In contrast, the members of a cooperative have strong incentives to exercise control over their cooperative. The services that members receive from their cooperative are often critical services that members are unable to receive, or cannot receive affordably, from other sources. Because the cooperative's sole purpose is to provide products and services to its members, the members not only have an economic interest in the cooperative; the economic fortunes of the members and the cooperatives are also intertwined in many ways.

This linkage between the member and the cooperative, when combined with the one-member/one-vote principle, means that members not only have control, but also often have the incentive and the desire to exercise that control and ensure that their cooperative continues to meet their needs. Because each member has one vote, no member "gives up" on the ability to influence the cooperative because of a perception that the member has insufficient voting power to be meaningful, or that certain interest holders have overwhelming influence. It is our experience that the member of a cooperative not only has more ability to exert control over his or her cooperative, but also is more likely to exercise the right to vote and affect the cooperative's operations. Understanding these aspects of the member/cooperative relationship is important to understanding what differentiates the cooperative from other business entities.

B. Directors

Although the ultimate control of a cooperative may rest with the cooperative's members, the responsibility for setting the policies and goals of a cooperative and for the selection and direction of management rests with the cooperative's board of directors. The directors serve as the elected representatives of the membership of the cooperative. As with the directors of a traditional corporation, the directors of the cooperative have authority only as a body, and not as individual directors.

The state statutes under which the cooperative is formed, together with common law, establish the responsibilities of the cooperative's board of directors. These responsibilities include representing the interest of the members as a whole and managing the affairs of the cooperative.[1] Although in most cooperatives the board of directors delegates the daily governance of the cooperative to professional management, such as a manager or chief executive officer (CEO), the board of directors retains the responsibility for the overall direction of the cooperative. For example, it is the board's responsibility to set the long-term and short-term strategic direction for the cooperative, while the manager or CEO is charged with implementing the strategy established by the board. In that sense, the responsibilities of the cooperative board are very much like that of the board of directors of any for-profit entity.

As with the director of a for-profit company, a primary responsibility of the cooperative director is the fiduciary obligation that the director owes to the organization and its members. This fiduciary obligation is an obligation of trust and imposes on one having such an obligation the requirement to act primarily for the benefit of another. The director's fiduciary obligation manifests itself in three specific duties: the duty of obedience, the duty of care, and the duty of loyalty. These duties are examined in more detail in the following.

1. Selection and Compensation

While the responsibilities of the directors of a cooperative are similar to the responsibilities of the directors of other business entities, the selection and compensation of cooperative directors is distinctive, and is often determined by the state statutory scheme under which the cooperative operates. The director of a typical corporation is selected on the basis of particular business expertise or success in another field of endeavor, and is usually compensated on the basis of market factors. While it is critical that a cooperative director have a sufficient degree of business acumen and an understanding of the industry in which the cooperative functions, additional criteria govern his or her selection to the cooperative board.

In many states, cooperative statutes require directors to be members of the cooperative (or, in the case of a federated cooperative, a member of a member of the cooperative),[2] although under some statutes the cooperative's bylaws can provide otherwise.[3] For example, under some state statutes, the cooperative's bylaws can provide that a specified number or percentage of directors can be nonmembers.[4] In most cases, the bylaws are drafted to specify that such directors serve only in an advisory capacity and have no voting rights, even though the applicable statute might allow such directors to have the same powers and rights as member directors.[5]

Some state cooperative statutes impose additional restrictions concerning the selection of directors, either directly or by allowing the cooperative's bylaws to contain such restrictions. For example, the Georgia Electric Membership Corporation Act allows directors to be elected by districts,[6] and the bylaws of many electric cooperatives in Georgia provide that a director must be a member of the district from which he or she is elected. Other state cooperative statutes allow cooperatives to provide similar requirements in their bylaws.[7] For someone unfamiliar with cooperatives, these restrictions may seem unusual and overly restrictive. When one considers the unity between customer and owner and the historical link between cooperatives and democratic control, such restrictions, whether imposed by statute or the cooperative's bylaws, seem both logical and desirable.

Compensation of cooperative directors is also subject to restrictions that do not typically apply to compensation of directors of other business entities. As already mentioned, compensation for directors of other organizations is typically market based; that is, directors are compensated based on a market assessment of the value of their contribution to the organization and the risks associated with serving on a corporate board. In contrast, under many cooperative statutes, compensation of directors is subject to limitations and restrictions. For example, some state statutes provide that cooperative directors can receive reimbursement only for actual expenses incurred plus a per diem payment.[8] Other statutes also allow reimbursement for additional expenses, such as insurance,[9] or allow directors to receive reimbursement of both fees and expenses.[10] Even where state statutes do not impose a monetary cap, as a practical matter, the members' control of the cooperative and their interest in its operations will impose a "reasonableness" cap on compensation.

2. Distinctive Characteristics of the Cooperative Board

As mentioned earlier, the responsibilities of the cooperative board are similar in many respects to the responsibilities of boards of for-profit corporations. However, the directors of cooperatives also face unique challenges that spring from the unique characteristics of the cooperative. While a complete identification and examination of these unique challenges is beyond the scope of this chapter, we will now examine several specific examples.

One challenge faced by the cooperative director arises from the fact that the cooperative's owners are also customers of the cooperative. This unity of owner and customer creates a difficult balance for many cooperative directors. For example, from the perspective of the owner of a corporation, it is in the best interests of the corporation to charge prices for the company's product or service that will create a financially strong entity. The interests of the customer need not be considered, except to the extent the corporation must perform market studies to discover the price customers are willing to pay. In contrast, the prices charged by the cooperative must take into account not only the health of the entity, but the interest of the members/customers in receiving the product or service at the lowest cost possible. Some types of cooperatives struggle more with this balance than others. For instance, the product provided by an electric cooperative is both essential and relatively expensive to provide, but the cooperative's board must insure that prices will result in a financially strong entity that can obtain the capital necessary to provide for power supply and essential capital assets.

Another set of challenges arises from the nonprofit nature of most cooperatives. As discussed earlier, cooperative members are not participating in the cooperative to achieve return on their investment. In contrast, the board of a for-profit corporation is aware that it is being judged by how well the board and management provide a sufficient return on investment for the shareholders, thus giving board members benchmarks against which to govern their performance and management's performance. A cooperative board does not have such a return on investment benchmark against which to govern its performance.

While it is true that lenders to cooperatives typically place financial covenants in the cooperative's debt instruments that provide certain minimum financial ratios, as a practical matter these ratios are not considered by the members in considering the board's performance, and are not helpful in assisting the board in setting financial goals that will satisfy the members. Judging the performance of a cooperative board is thus necessarily much more subjective than judging the performance of a corporate board.

Certain structural aspects of the cooperative also make it difficult to bring an objective viewpoint to particular business issues. In cases where directors of a cooperative are elected by geographic district, a director from a district might face a conflict where a course of action that is in the best interest of the cooperative as a whole does not necessarily best serve the district from which the director was elected. However, the director is called on to make decisions that best serve the cooperative, as opposed to individual customers (including the director) or groups of customers (such as members in the director's district).

More complex conflicts can arise where federated cooperatives are involved, since it is typical for directors of the federated cooperative to also be directors on the boards of the local cooperatives that are members of the federated cooperative. In such a case, how does a director who serves at both levels separate the need to act in the best interests of the federated cooperative as a whole from the obligation to act in the best interest of the local cooperative? Also, how does the director deal with privileged or confidential information obtained from the federated cooperative when acting as director of the local cooperative? As one can see, there are no universal answers to dealing with such issues. Each conflict has to be evaluated on the basis of the particular facts and the applicable state law.

3. Liability and Training

As demonstrated by the many news stories over the last few years concerning civil and criminal actions against corporate directors, the role of the board of directors in corporate governance has come under intense scrutiny, and boards that were once content to delegate most of their responsibilities to management are being advised to carefully consider their role and their potential liability for failing to "mind the store." At this time, the legal measures imposed to improve standards of accountability, such as the Sarbanes-Oxley Act of 2002, apply only to large, publicly traded corporations. Nonetheless, even though not required to do so, many larger cooperatives are adopting similar standards in an attempt to incorporate "best practices" in the governance of the cooperative. Such cooperatives are likely mindful of the movements in some states to apply the requirements imposed by the Sarbanes-Oxley Act to large nonprofit organizations as well, including cooperatives.

One result of the increased scrutiny on the cooperative board of directors is an increased awareness of the need for seminars and educational programs for cooperative boards. Directors are now expected to have more than a passing understanding of financial statements, their fiduciary responsibilities to the cooperative, and other essential items. Many trade associations associated with cooperatives already provide comprehensive training programs for cooperative directors. For example, the National Rural Electric Cooperative Association, the national trade association for electric cooperatives, provides a comprehensive series of training programs for cooperative directors involved in the rural electric cooperative program, while the Credit Union National Association offers training for credit union directors. In addition, most states have statewide trade associations associated with various categories of cooperatives that provide director training and support. As an example, in Texas the Texas Agricultural Cooperative Council offers training programs for agricultural cooperatives. Also, colleges and universities across the country have developed cooperative development centers that publish helpful background and training materials for the cooperative director.[11]

As discussed in the following, the continued focus on corporate governance increases the risk that directors may face personal liability arising from their duties on the board. Ultimately, the best protection against personal liability comes from having knowledgeable board members that are prepared to ask questions of management, educate themselves about the cooperative's affairs, and retain capable advisors familiar with cooperatives, such as accountants and attorneys. With some issues, reliance on advisors is essential, especially when directors make decisions related to employment, securities, tax and antitrust issues. In addition, maintaining good communication with the cooperative's members can eliminate misunderstandings that could possibly lead to claims. For example, because directors are called upon to make decisions as to distribution of dividends and retention and distribution of patronage refunds, directors should ensure that members are aware of the cooperative's policies on such issues.

C. Officers and Management

While the nature of the cooperative structure often results in the cooperative's board of directors taking a more active role in the management of the cooperative than is typically found in the traditional corporation, the day-to-day affairs of a cooperative are generally delegated to a CEO or manager. In some cases the manager's role is specified in the bylaws, in others the board establishes the manager's duties through a board resolution. In all cases, however, the manager has the often difficult, and sometimes conflicting, responsibilities of satisfying the members and meeting the expectations of the board of directors.

With the exception of the manager/CEO, the senior officers of a cooperative, such as the president and vice president, often come from among the members of the board of directors. Although some cooperative statutes allow for the election of particular officers by the cooperative's members,[12] the officers of a cooperative are typically elected by the board of directors and serve at the pleasure of the board.[13] As with the traditional corporation, the officers of a cooperative have such duties as are provided in the cooperative's bylaws and the statutes governing the particular type of cooperative, as well as the duties specified by the board of directors. In addition, the officers of the cooperative, like the officers of the traditional corporation, have those implied duties typically associated with one holding a particular office.

In cooperatives in which the manager is also designated as the CEO, the president, vice president, and other officers are typically members of the board, while the manager/CEO is not. If the manager is given the title of president, the senior officers serving on the board may be designated as chairman and vice chairman. The manager/CEO typically is responsible for hiring the cooperative's other employees, and depending on the size of the cooperative, the manager/CEO may also be given the authority to hire other officers to manage the cooperative, such as vice presidents to head various business functions or departments. In smaller cooperatives, the manager might not be an officer of the corporation, but might instead report to the president of the board of directors. The bylaws of some cooperatives do not require the manager to be a member of the cooperative. In fact, some cooperatives' bylaws expressly prohibit the manager from being a member of the cooperative.

Like cooperative directors, officers of cooperatives typically face a different set of challenges than officers of traditional corporations. For example, while the CEO of a corporation and the manager of the cooperative are both responsible for communications with the owners of the entity, the cooperative's members, unlike the corporation's shareholders, have a far greater, and more personal, interest in the quality and value of the products sold by the cooperative and the cooperative's quality of service. Also, especially in smaller cooperatives, the manager is more likely to face searching questions from members about products, expenses, employees, the state of the business, and management practices. In many cases, managers ensure that there are member appreciation days, periodic newsletters, and other avenues of direct communication with members. And, of course, as with the typical corporation, the cooperative provides an official report to members at its annual meeting.

Just as with directors, training is available for cooperative officers. Every cooperative has a vested interest in ensuring that its officers are familiar with their duties to the cooperative and with the federal, state, and local laws applicable to the cooperative and its operations. In turn, the management team of the cooperative is often given the responsibility of arranging training for new cooperative directors. Although, as discussed, most of the new laws and regulations aimed at corporate boards and management do not apply to cooperatives, in recognition of the changing standards brought about by recent examples of corporate malfeasance, many cooperatives are increasing their emphasis on training programs and are putting new "best practices" in place.

D. The Duties of Officers and Directors

Officers and directors of a cooperative owe a fiduciary duty to the cooperative, just as the officers and directors of the traditional corporation owe a fiduciary duty to their corporation. Courts examining the concept of fiduciary duty often begin with the definition of *fiduciary* provided by Black's Law Dictionary:

> [A] person holding the character of a trustee, or a character analogous to that of a trustee, with respect to the trust and confidence involved in it and the scrupulous good faith and candor which it requires. A person having the duty, created by his undertaking, to act primarily for another's benefit in matters connected with such undertaking.[14]

In short, a fiduciary duty is the highest standard of care.

What specific duties are encompassed by the fiduciary duties owed to the cooperative? Put another way, what must the cooperative's officers and directors do to fulfill their fiduciary duties? Although courts and commentators place different labels on these duties, they can generally be placed in three categories: (1) duty of loyalty; (2) duty of care; and (3) duty of obedience. While a few cases have addressed the duties of directors and officers of cooperatives, courts and commentators typically turn to principles of corporate law for guidance when specific cooperative case law is unavailable.

1. Duty of Care

Officers and directors first of all owe a duty of care to the cooperative members and to the cooperative itself. Whether provided by statute or under common law, this duty requires the officer or director to discharge his or her duties in good faith, and with the care an ordinary prudent person would exercise under similar circumstances.[15] This duty encompasses a duty to be diligent in attending to the affairs of the cooperative and to inquire as to matters affecting the cooperative. Officers and directors are held accountable both for what they know and what they should know and are required to find out the information necessary for them to carry out their duties.

As part of the duty of care, the cooperative officer or director is required to actively participate in the matters of the cooperative and to stay informed about the cooperative's business in general. Directors must make a particular effort in this regard, since they are less engaged with the cooperative's affairs on a daily basis. Directors must regularly attend meetings, prepare for those meetings and meaningfully participate in those meetings. As stated by the New York Court of Appeals almost 100 years ago when discussing directors' duties, "No custom or practice can make a directorship a mere position of honor void of responsibility, or cause a name to become a substitute for care and attention. The personnel of a directorate may give confidence and attract custom; it must also afford protection."[16]

While the director can under certain circumstances meet the duty of care by relying on the expertise of others, such as accountants or attorneys, the director must still exercise his or her independent and informed judgment on matters brought before the board with the objective of acting in the best interest of all members of the cooperative. A director may not rely solely on the judgment of other directors or take direction from others, including individual members of the cooperative. This is the case even where the director is on the board of a federated cooperative and also sits on the board of one of its member cooperatives. Such a director, when acting in his capacity as a director of the federated cooperative, cannot take direction from the member cooperative or consider the particular interests of the member cooperative to the detriment of the membership as a whole.

2. Duty of Loyalty

Officers and directors also owe a duty of loyalty to the cooperative. A decision from the New York courts provides an excellent synopsis of the responsibilities a director (and, by analogy, an officer), must carry out in fulfilling his or her duty of loyalty:

> It is clear that a director owes loyalty and allegiance to the company— a loyalty that is undivided and an allegiance that is influenced in action by no consideration other than the welfare of the corporation. Any adverse interest of a director will be subjected to a scrutiny rigid and uncompromising. He may not profit at the expense of his corporation and in conflict with its rights; he may not for personal gain divert unto himself the opportunities which in equity and fairness belong to his corporation. He is required to use his independent judgment.[17]

The officers and directors are thus required to act in the cooperative's best interests and put aside personal or conflicting interests when making decisions for or acting on behalf of the cooperative.

Most cooperatives have policies concerning conflicting interest transactions by officers and directors. Such transactions include contracts or transactions between the cooperative and an officer or director or an entity in which the officer or director has an interest. Although some state business corporation statutes contain provisions governing conflicting interests, most cooperative statutes do not, and officers and directors typically must draw guidance from state decisions addressing corporations.

The member/cooperative relationship raises conflict of interest questions that typically do not arise in the corporate context. Most directors on cooperative boards are also members of the cooperative, and thus the typical director will have an inherent economic interest in most matters that come before the board. It would be infeasible for directors to refrain from taking part in every decision that dealt with matters in which the directors had a financial interest. The special structure of the cooperative must be taken into account when considering conflicts of interest. When a director is considering matters that affect the economic interests of all members, including the director, it would seem that no conflict of interest would exist. On the other hand, if the transaction in question would benefit the director as compared to other members, then a conflict of interest analysis would have to be performed.

The mere fact that a transaction involves a conflict of interest does not make it voidable or subject to enjoinment. Many transactions involving conflicting interests can pass muster provided that full disclosure is made to the board of directors or the transaction, judged as of the time it was entered into, is shown to be fair to the cooperative. Nevertheless, to avoid any appearance of impropriety and the possibility of litigation, many cooperative policies forbid or severely restrict conflicting interest transactions.

As part of the duty of loyalty, officers and directors have the responsibility to act in the best interest of the cooperative and in the best interest of the cooperative's membership as a whole. We have discussed earlier that the nature of the cooperative often makes it difficult for an officer or director to determine which course of action is in the best interest of the membership as a whole, and to balance the interest of the cooperative as an entity with that of the interests of its individual members. In some cases, the applicable state statute might specifically provide the factors that a director may consider in determining what is in the best interests of the cooperative. For example, a Wisconsin statute provides that a director may consider the effect of a proposed action on employees and customers, the communities in which the cooperative operates, the cooperative's members, the long-term and short-term interests of the cooperative and its members, and other factors the director considers pertinent.[18] On the other hand, when considering specific groups, officers and directors must avoid taking action with the intent of enhancing the interests of one group at the expense of another. The duty of loyalty can be violated by unequal treatment of members, especially if the officer or director involved in the decision is a member of the group being benefitted.

The requirement to act in the best interest of the cooperative raises interesting issues in the case of federated cooperatives. For example, in the case of a generation and transmission cooperative that furnishes power to its member distribution cooperatives, directors are often called upon to vote for rate increases. These directors typically also serve on the board of the member distribution cooperatives. While the rate increases might be required to keep the generation and transmission cooperative financially healthy, such rate increases will automatically increase costs for the distribution cooperatives. However, the duty of loyalty requires such directors, when making such decisions, to consider the best interests of the generation and transmission cooperative.

The duty of loyalty thus requires officers and directors to

- refrain from deriving personal benefits from the cooperative not made available to other members;
- avoid granting privileges or benefits to one group of members at the expense of other members;
- avoid discriminating against certain members or groups of members;
- properly handle conflicts of interest, by refraining from using the position of officer or director or using the cooperative's assets for personal gain or engaging in a competing interest; and
- act in good faith in all relations with the cooperative.

3. Duty of Obedience

In meeting their duty of obedience to the cooperative, officers and directors must act in furtherance of the cooperative's stated business purpose and follow the bylaws and policies of the cooperative and all applicable federal and state laws, including tax and employment laws. As with the duty of care, this duty typically requires reliance upon outside advisors, such as attorneys and accountants.

4. Minimizing Liability

The state enabling statute typically allows the cooperative, through its bylaws, to eliminate or limit the personal liability of the officer or director to the cooperative for a breach of fiduciary duty; however, the cooperative is generally not allowed to do so with respect to breach of the duty of loyalty or care, for bad faith, intentional misconduct, or transaction from which the director or officer derives an improper personal benefit.[19] Importantly, directors are entitled to rely on opinions and information, including financial statements, prepared by officers, attorneys, accountants, and so on, and state statutes typically provide that a director who does so in good faith cannot be held liable for any actions or omissions in his or her performance as a director.[20]

What practical steps can a cooperative take to minimize liability of the cooperative and its board for the actions taken by officers and directors? The cooperative can make efforts to provide thorough communications to members concerning important decisions taken by the cooperative and its board. The cooperative, through its CEO/manager, should also ensure that incoming directors receive training concerning the duties of the cooperative board, and that directors receive all necessary information required for making decisions as a board. It is important for the board of directors to maintain correct and thorough minutes of all meetings and to document how and why decisions were reached. Also, the board should document any reliance placed on advisors, such as attorneys and accountants. Board members should make an effort to actively participate in the cooperative's affairs, faithfully attend board meetings, ensure that accurate minutes of board meetings are taken and formally approved, and maintain a general knowledge of the cooperative's books and records, such as accounting records, the bylaws, and tax returns. Finally, the cooperative should have appropriate policies in place, including policies concerning independent audits, internal controls, and conflicting interest transactions.

Even if an action is brought on the basis of decisions made by the cooperative's officers and directors, just as with the typical corporation, many decisions of officers and directors are protected by the business judgment rule. In some states, the business judgment rule is codified by statute; in others its contours are established by common law. The business judgment rule essentially protects officers and directors from direct liability for decisions made in good faith and with due care that further legitimate purposes of the cooperative, even where such decisions might be viewed as the "wrong" decision with the benefit of hindsight. It is intended to provide officers and directors the latitude to take risks necessary to fulfill the cooperative's purposes without the constant fear of lawsuits challenging unsuccessful decisions. The rule does so by imposing a presumption that decisions made are consistent with officers' and directors' fiduciary duties as long as they are supported by a rational business purpose.

The business judgment rule thus places the burden on the plaintiff to show evidence that the officers or directors violated their fiduciary duties. The extent of this burden, and the factors considered by the court, vary depending on applicable state law. Ultimately the plaintiff's burden is to show that the decision made was not supported by any rational business purpose, or, as some courts have stated, to show that the decision was so far beyond the bounds of reasonable judgment that it is inexplicable on any ground other than bad faith. Certain decisions, such as pricing, negotiating credit terms, and employment relations, are typically protected by the business judgment rule, and plaintiffs face a difficult burden in overcoming the presumptions accompanying the rule. Plaintiffs face greater success in attacking decisions that clearly fall outside the cooperative's bylaws or policies, such as decisions that bypass accounting controls or demonstrate a conflict of interest.

A note of caution follows regarding the business judgment rule: the scope of the rule's protection varies from state to state, and in some states, such as Delaware, court decisions have resulted in state legislative action that affects the rule's scope as well. In addition, because most court cases and statutes address the rule in the corporate context, care must be taken when analyzing the application of the rule in the cooperative context.

5. Liability, Indemnity and Insurance

What protections can officers and directors obtain against the potential liability that accompanies the job? To the extent allowed by state statute, the cooperative can indemnify officers and directors against personal liability and can agree in advance to pay litigation costs, settlements and judgments on the director's behalf. As is the case with officers and directors of corporations, this protection is not absolute. State statutes limit the types of conduct for which indemnification is available; for example, most statutes provide that the cooperative cannot indemnify an officer or director for a claim resulting from fraud or intentional misconduct. Also, the cooperative may choose to impose additional restrictions in its bylaws, or elect not to provide indemnification. Finally, if the cooperative is itself insolvent or experiencing financial trouble, the officer or director facing a lawsuit will derive little comfort from indemnification unless an insurance policy provides coverage.

Some states have enacted statutes that provide directors and managers of cooperatives with increased protection from liability. For example, under North Dakota's electric cooperative act and general cooperative act, directors, officers and managers are immune from civil liability for acts or omissions in the course of their duties unless gross negligence or willful misconduct was involved.[21] A Tennessee statute provides similar protection, and also limits the time to bring an action for breach of fiduciary duty to one year.[22] The theory behind such statutes is that, in light of the limited compensation for directors of cooperatives and other nonprofit associations, some protection for liability should be provided to ensure that qualified candidates seek such positions.

Cooperatives can also provide protection for directors and officers by purchasing a directors and officers liability insurance policy, typically referred to as D & O insurance. Such policies provide coverage for certain acts committed or alleged to have been committed by the directors and officers of the cooperative, and might cover both claims that the cooperative is required to indemnify and non-indemnified claims. Coverage is not absolute, however, and policies typically exclude claims alleging fraud, criminal acts, acts that harm the cooperative, such as self-dealing, and bodily injury, and property damage. Some state cooperative statutes specifically authorize the cooperative to purchase and maintain liability insurance that provides protection for acts and omissions of directors and officers, even those for which the director or officer would not be entitled to indemnification.[23] In any event, obtaining insurance would likely be authorized under the general purposes and powers of the cooperative.

E. Contractual Relationships Between the Cooperative and Its Members

As we have seen, once a cooperative is formed, the relationship between the cooperative and its members is defined by several sources, including state law and the cooperative's bylaws and articles of incorporation. Under the common law of most states, the bylaws are deemed to create a contractual relationship between the cooperative and its members. For some types of cooperatives, these sources, together with the guidance of the board and management, are sufficient. In contrast, other cooperatives require that members enter into a formal contractual relationship with the cooperative. This is particularly true of marketing cooperatives, utility cooperatives, and "new age" cooperatives. For these types of cooperatives, the contract with the members is a fundamental building block that allows the cooperative to obtain financing and commence operations.

Agricultural marketing cooperatives typically require their members to execute a marketing agreement under which the cooperative is given the exclusive right to purchase commodities from the member and sell them through the cooperative. Having such exclusive contracts in place gives the cooperative at least some ability to depend on a steady supply of products to sell to third parties and to make financial forecasts based on the predicated volume of commodities. Agricultural supply cooperatives often require exclusive contracts as well. Because the marketing agreement plays such an important role in ensuring the success of the marketing cooperative, the marketing cooperative acts in many states specifically allow for such agreements and set forth parameters for the marketing agreement.[24] For example, Colorado's cooperative statute allows agricultural cooperatives to enter into exclusive marketing or purchasing contracts with their members, provided such contracts have a term of ten years or less.[25] The cooperative statutes in Hawaii and Iowa have similar restrictions.[26] The cooperative statutes in Alaska, Colorado, and other states allow cooperatives to provide liquidated damages provisions in member contracts that require members to pay liquidated damages to the cooperative in the event of breach.[27]

"New generation cooperatives," which in many ways are a type of marketing cooperative, place even greater emphasis on the contract between the cooperative and its members, primarily because of the capital-intensive nature of such cooperatives. In addition to requiring exclusivity, the member contracts obligate members to deliver a specified quantity of the commodity to the cooperative each year. The contracts typically impose quality or grade requirements as well. If the member does not fulfill this obligation and delivers less than the specified amount, or delivers commodities that do not meet the quality requirements, the contract gives the cooperative the right to buy the remaining amount on the open market and to require the member to pay the difference in price. New generation cooperatives are discussed in more detail in Chapter II.

Utility cooperatives, such as electric and telephone cooperatives, also typically require their members to enter into contracts with the cooperatives. For example, most electric distribution electric cooperatives (the cooperatives that sell power directly to the end user) enter into an all-requirements wholesale power contract with their federated generation and transmission cooperative. Under this model, the distribution cooperative acts as the local distributor and primary customer contact. The federated generation and transmission cooperative, which is owned and controlled by its members, the distribution cooperatives, provides a centralized focus for the development of necessary generation and transmission resources used to generate and deliver power to the distribution cooperatives for ultimate delivery to the consumer/member. Under the all-requirements contract, the distribution cooperative commits to buy all of its power and transmission services during the time of the wholesale contract from the generation and transmission cooperative.

This wholesale power contract not only serves as a necessary part of most electric cooperative structures but has in fact been a primary building block of the rural electric cooperative program. This form of all-requirements contract is generally required by the Rural Utilities Service of the Department of Agriculture as the primary security for loans that allow cooperatives to develop necessary generation and transmission resources. Without the cooperative's members' commitment to pay for the generation and transmission resources built with the government's loans and loan guarantees, it is difficult to see how electric cooperatives would attract the capital necessary to build the required generation and transmission.

Notes

1. *See, e.g.*, Alaska Stat. § 10.15.140; Kan. Stat. Ann. § 17-1611; Ky. Rev. Stat. Ann. § 272.171; Neb. Rev. Stat. § 70-718.
2. Alaska Stat. § 10.25.140; O.C.G.A. § 46-5-82; Kan. Stat. Ann. § 17-4661.
3. *See* Ariz. Rev. Stat. Ann. § 10-2058.
4. *See* Colo. Rev. Stat. § 7-56-401.
5. N.H. Rev. Stat. Ann. § 301:18.

6. O.C.G.A. § 46-3-293(e).
7. Ala. Code § 2-10-60; Cal. Food & Agric. Code § 54142.
8. *See* O.C.G.A. § 46-3-290(d) (electric cooperatives); O.C.G.A. § 46-5-82 (telephone cooperatives).
9. Alaska Stat. § 10.25.140.
10. Ariz. Rev. Stat. Ann. § 10-2058; Kan. Stat. Ann. § 17-4661.
11. For example, the University of Wisconsin Center for Cooperatives offers a wide variety of publications and programs, including training programs for directors and managers. *See* http://www.uwcc.wisc.edu.
12. *See* O.C.G.A. § 46-03-301(b).
13. N.Y. Coop. Corp. Law § 64.
14. BLACK'S LAW DICTIONARY 625 (6th ed. 1990).
15. *See* Tenn. Code Ann. § 43-38-616(a); O.C.G.A. § 46-3-303.1; Wis. Stat. Ann. § 193.455.
16. Kavanaugh v. Commonwealth Trust Co., 119 N.E. 237, 238 (N.Y. 1918).
17. Litwin v. Allen, 25 N.Y.S.2d 667, 677 (N.Y. Sup. Ct. 1940).
18. Wis. Stat. Ann. § 193.455; Iowa Code. Ann. § 501A.712.
19. Utah Code Ann. § 3-1-13.1; Wis. Stat. Ann. § 193.465; Wyo. Stat. Ann. § 17-10-220.
20. Tenn. Code. Ann. § 43-38-616.
21. N.D. Cent. Code §§ 10-13-10 & 10-15-31; S.C. Code Ann. §§ 33-31-834 & 33-46-520. *See also* Utah Code Ann. § 3-1-13.3 (agricultural cooperatives).
22. Tenn. Code Ann. § 48-58-601.
23. *See* Alaska Stat. § 10.25.145(c) (electric and telephone cooperatives).
24. Md. Code Ann., Corps. & Ass'ns § 5-552.
25. Colo. Rev. Stat. § 7-56-502.
26. Haw. Rev. Stat. § 421-18; Iowa Code Ann. § 501A.603.
27. Alaska Stat. § 10.15.220; Colo. Rev. Stat. § 7-56-503.

Further Reading

Director Liability in Agricultural Cooperatives, USDA COOPERATIVE INFORMATION REPORT NO. 34 (1996).

Comment, *Board of Directors' Fiduciary Duties: Are They Compromised in Agricultural Cooperatives?,* 10 SAN JOAQUIN AGRIC. L. REV. 201 (2000).

VI

Capitalization and Finance

While some aspects of the capitalization and financing of cooperatives will be familiar to the practitioner conversant with other types of business entities, certain features are unique to cooperatives and are very different from comparable characteristics of cooperatives' corporate counterparts. As we will see, these unique features are a natural consequence of the cooperative principles and structure. This chapter will discuss the differences between stock and nonstock cooperatives, the function and use of equity and debt capital, the cooperative's treatment of net earnings, including retention and distribution of net earnings, and the equity redemption plans under which retained earnings are periodically returned to the cooperative's members.

A. Comparison of Stock Cooperatives and Nonstock Cooperatives

Cooperatives can be classified as either stock cooperatives or nonstock cooperatives. Simply put, in a stock cooperative, shares are issued to the cooperative's members, while in a nonstock cooperative, membership certificates are issued to the members. Put another way, a person or entity becomes a member of a cooperative, with an accompanying voting right, through the purchase and possession of the stock certificate or membership certificate.

Modern cooperative statutes (those enacted beginning in the twentieth century) often allow for the formation of both stock and nonstock cooperatives. Both classifications sound familiar to the general practitioner: stock cooperatives invite comparison with the ordinary corporation and its issuance of shares, while nonstock cooperatives resemble in some respects the nonprofit corporation with membership classes. Although the differences between stock and nonstock cooperatives will be discussed in this chapter, in practice there are few operational differences between the two models.

In many cases how the cooperative is organized is dependent on the requirements of the applicable state statute.

1. Stock Cooperatives

Stock cooperatives, like ordinary corporations, issue common shares and, in some cases, preferred shares. In the ordinary corporation, shares of common stock are in general subject to few restrictions, although shareholders may agree to restrictions on the transfer of the corporation's shares, and certain restrictions may be imposed under state and federal law, such as the securities laws. In a stock cooperative, however, shares typically carry multiple restrictions, including restrictions on transferability, rate of return, and voting rights. As with ordinary corporations, stock cooperatives may divide both common and preferred stock into classes and may assign different par values to or impose different restrictions on such classes.

Common stock. The cooperative principles limit return on equity capital. This principle of limited return on investment is based on the assumption that the primary purpose of the cooperative is to provide members with needed goods or services, rather than to provide return on investment. Many state laws limit dividends paid by cooperatives to no more than eight percent per year. Unlike the common stock of an ordinary corporation, cooperative common stock is limited in the rate of return available for shareholders. In any event, most cooperatives do not pay any dividend at all on common stock.

Cooperative principles require restrictions on transferability of common stock, since otherwise shares, and possibly control, of the cooperative could be transferred to nonmembers who do not use the cooperative's goods or services. In the typical large corporation, where an individual shareholder has little power over the affairs of the corporation, there is little concern over how or when such a shareholder transfers his or her shares. Unless the shareholders agree to restrict transfer through a shareholder agreement or through some other mechanism, shares are usually freely transferable. In contrast, the cooperative has a great interest in how shares may be transferred because of the importance of member control. Also, in cases where voting rights are based on the number of shares owned, restrictions may be placed on a member's sale of shares to other members in order to preserve the one-member/one-vote requirement. As one court observed when analyzing the characteristics of cooperative shares, "A growth stock would be a rank misnomer for such a security."[1]

Voting rights of common shares are also restricted, in that each member is typically limited to one vote, and does not have voting rights proportional to ownership of shares. The voting restriction, which typically is embedded in the applicable state statutory scheme, and may also be required in connection with certain federal tax laws, arises from one of the primary principles of cooperatives, which is to ensure democratic member control. This principle is intended to result in an organization in which a broad spectrum of the members participate in directing the cooperative's activities and making policy decisions for the cooperative.

In some states, such as Alaska, New York, and Florida, certain types of cooperatives may provide for voting rights in proportion to the volume of business that the member does with the cooperative; that is, voting on a patronage basis.[2] Some states allow additional forms of voting rights. For example, in Vermont, a marketing cooperative's bylaws may provide members with voting rights in proportion to the land leased by members for use in producing products handled by the cooperative.[3] In any case, the cooperative's bylaws (and where required by state law, its articles of incorporation) should specify the voting rights of common stock.

In the early days of the modern cooperative, the one-member/one-vote requirement worked well for all cooperatives, which tended to be fairly small and local in nature. With the emergence of federated cooperatives, the requirement has been changed for purposes of voting on the affairs of the federated cooperative. For example, some federated cooperatives are governed by a board of directors elected on a regional basis by representatives of the member cooperatives. Some state statutory schemes have been revised to accommodate different voting structures for federated cooperatives.[4] For our purposes in this chapter, however, we can assume that for the typical centralized cooperative, each member is typically limited to one vote, regardless of the amount of common stock owned.

Preferred stock. The typical cooperative does not generate the majority, or even a sizable portion, of its capital from the sale of common stock to its members. In many cooperatives, where membership is conditioned upon buying one share of common stock, a share costs only a few hundred dollars and carries no dividend. The cooperative has another option for investment by members (and in some cases by nonmembers as well): the sale of preferred shares. As with the preferred shares issued by an ordinary corporation, a cooperative's preferred shares provide a fixed annual yield, carry no voting rights, and carry a preference over common shares in the event of liquidation of the cooperative. In most states the yield of preferred shares is limited to eight percent per year. The cooperative may elect whether the shares will be cumulative (with dividends not paid in one year due and payable in subsequent years) or noncumulative (with the cooperative not responsible for subsequent payment of missed dividends). The cooperative may also elect to provide a redemption right whereby the board of directors may choose to redeem preferred shares by repaying the shareholders a stated price.

In some states there are statutory restrictions on the transferability of preferred stock. However, in some cases (where allowed by law), preferred stock is freely transferable among members, and cooperatives may sell or allow transfer of preferred shares to nonmembers of the cooperative. For example, in Florida, the preferred stock of agricultural marketing cooperatives may be sold to nonmembers.[5] Such sales do not violate the cooperative principle of democratic control since preferred shares in such cases do not carry voting rights, and thus, nonmembers cannot attain control of the cooperative or direct its policies.

Under the right circumstances, the sale of preferred shares to nonmembers can benefit the cooperative by providing an additional source of capital and by giving opportunities for interested individuals in the community to participate in the success of the cooperative. In the typical cooperative, such benefits have been limited by the eight percent cap on dividends, since nonmembers have typically found it more beneficial, at least from an economic standpoint, to invest in other opportunities.

2. Nonstock Cooperatives

The membership interest in a nonstock cooperative is memorialized by a membership certificate rather than by common shares. The member receives a membership certificate upon payment of a membership fee and receives no interest on such fees paid. In many cases there is little difference between this process and the issuance of shares, since most cooperatives do not pay dividends on common stock. Nonstock cooperatives rarely obtain much of their capital requirements from membership fees because such fees are usually low and are not intended to contribute significantly to capital requirements.

While a stock cooperative raises additional capital through the sale of preferred stock, the nonstock cooperative does so through the sale of capital certificates, which have many of the characteristics of preferred stock. Capital certificates usually do not carry voting rights and have a fixed rate of return. It is preferable for the cooperative to have the power to retire such capital certificates or for such certificates to have a due date for redemption. As with preferred stock, where allowed by law, such capital certificates may be sold to nonmembers of the cooperative.

In practice, after the initial organization of the cooperative, there are few differences between the stock and the nonstock cooperative. The previous discussion in connection with stock cooperatives as to voting rights, limitations on transfer, and so on, applies equally to nonstock cooperatives.

B. Capital

As with any business, a cooperative, once organized, requires capital to begin operations, with that capital consisting of (1) equity capital (sometimes referred to as member equity), which includes capital contributed by the members and nonmembers of the cooperative, and (2) debt capital, consisting of money borrowed by the cooperative. Members forming a smaller cooperative might be able to supply most of the cooperative's initial capital needs and, thus, avoid the need to incur debt. However, the traditional cooperative usually meets only a portion of its needs through the initial equity capital that it raises, especially as additional capital is needed to fund the cooperative's growth. The cooperative's members thus must consider not only how to meet the cooperative's initial capital needs, but also how to raise and manage additional capital to fund the cooperative's growth.

1. Equity Capital

The traditional cooperative obtains most of its equity capital from its members rather than from nonmembers. This is a necessary function of the nature of the cooperative, which in a sense operates as a flow-through entity to bring savings to its members, rather than as an entity devoted to generating profit for the benefit of shareholders. Where an ordinary corporation might attract investors on the strength of its business plan and future prospects, the cooperative's focus on its members, combined with the restrictions that accompany the cooperative form, make the traditional cooperative relatively unattractive to outside investors. These differences are perhaps not as distinct when cooperatives are compared to smaller companies, partnerships, or sole proprietorships, where business owners also face challenges in obtaining investment from third parties.

When starting a cooperative, deciding on the initial amount of equity capital to be contributed by the members is important, not only for finance, but also for the purpose of ensuring that members are sufficiently committed to the cooperative. If the members have a significant financial stake in the cooperative, they likely will be more active in using the cooperative's services and promoting the cooperative's success. Also, strong member equity ensures that creditors will not be given too much control over the cooperative's affairs.

It almost goes without saying that equity capital must also be sufficient to promote the financial well-being of the cooperative and its operations. Various rules of thumb have been published over the years concerning suitable levels of equity capital, such as requiring equity capital to be at least double the amount of debt capital. Of course it might be impossible for members of certain types of capital-intensive cooperatives to meet such rules of thumb. For example, electric and telephone cooperatives typically require incurring and carrying extensive debt to finance equipment, operations, infrastructure, and initial capital outlays.

The proportion of equity capital is also important because it determines the amount of financing that the cooperative can receive, as well as how favorable the terms of such financing will be. Most lenders to cooperatives require cooperatives to maintain a certain level of equity capital. As a consequence, loan documents typically contain restrictions and covenants that require the cooperative to comply with specified debt-to-equity ratios.

The cooperative determines how much initial equity capital it will receive by setting the purchase requirements for common stock or the amount required in payment for membership certificates. In some cases all members might be required to contribute the same amount of equity capital. In many cooperatives, voting rights are based on the amount of stock owned, and under the one-member/one-vote principle, each member purchases the same amount of shares. In other cases, the cooperative might elect to require contribution based on the member's expected volume of use of the cooperative's goods or services, or might require members to purchase additional shares based on an increase in patronage. In determining what the required equity capital contribution will be, however, the cooperative must forecast its initial capital needs by analyzing capital equipment costs, expected overhead, and other expected expenses.

Cooperatives can use preferred stock and capital certificates as a means of obtaining additional equity capital from members who wish to contribute more than their share. Even where cooperatives are permitted to sell preferred stock or capital certificates to nonmembers, however, the traditional cooperative typically obtains little, if any, equity capital from nonmembers. One significant difference between the cooperative and other business forms that dissuades nonmembers from investing is the fact that a cooperative's members receive net margins (net earnings) in proportion to their patronage (their level of business with the cooperative), rather than on the basis of their equity investment in the cooperative. Also, most cooperatives do not pay interest on equity capital, and in any event, state and federal laws typically limit dividends paid by cooperatives to eight percent. Because of these and other restrictions, such as restrictions on transferability, few nonmembers purchase preferred stock or capital certificates in a cooperative.

Allocated and unallocated equity capital. Equity capital must be allocated or unallocated. Simply put, allocated equity is equity capital assigned to the individual capital accounts of the cooperative's members, while unallocated equity is not assigned to a particular member's capital account, but is held by the cooperative for all members. The cooperative is required to return allocated equity to its members at some point in time. In contrast, unallocated equity is considered permanent capital of the cooperative, and the cooperative has no obligation to return unallocated equity to its members.

Allocated equity consists of equity capital that is assigned to members in proportion to their patronage—that is, the amount of business that members do with the cooperative. Allocated equity is built up by the cooperative in several ways: (1) retained earnings of the cooperative resulting from the members' business with the cooperative, to the extent allocated by the cooperative (referred to as retained margins or retained capital credits and further discussed later in this chapter); and (2) in the case of some marketing cooperatives, per-unit retains, also known as transaction retains, in which the cooperative retains a specified amount from each sale transaction that would otherwise be distributed to the member. In these instances, the members' capital accounts are credited for such capital contributions.

Although cooperatives could provide that such capital accounts will earn interest, in practice few cooperatives do so.

Unallocated equity is not allocated to members' individual capital accounts. Unallocated equity may have several sources, including money received from the sale of assets of the cooperative. (Cooperatives can also generate unallocated equity through the sale of preferred stock to nonmembers; however, as noted, few cooperatives do so.) Also, cooperatives typically elect to retain a portion of net margins as unallocated equity. Unlike allocated equity, which is paid back to the cooperative's members, unallocated equity is held by and for the benefit of the cooperative and is not paid back to members unless the cooperative dissolves or is liquidated. In such an event, distribution would be made in accordance with the cooperative's bylaws and with the governing state statute.

In some situations unallocated equity can be very beneficial for the cooperative, since the cooperative has more flexibility in how it uses unallocated equity. While allocated equity must be maintained for the individual members, the cooperative can use unallocated equity to replace allocated equity in emergencies or as a source to return members' equity capital on an accelerated schedule. Unallocated equity can be considered permanent capital, in the nature of reserves, and can also provide a source of working capital.

Equity capital in new generation cooperatives. Equity is usually managed differently in new generation cooperatives than in traditional cooperatives. Because new generation cooperatives typically require substantial initial amounts of capital to buy necessary processing equipment, they typically require substantial initial investments from their members. Also, to ensure the financial livelihood of the cooperative, in return for the member's equity investment the member typically receives shares that carry contractual rights and obligations to deliver a specified amount of product to the cooperative. Managing equity in a new generation cooperative presents additional issues that the traditional cooperative is not required to address. For example, the new generation cooperative might need the ability to require members to make additional capital contributions in the event the cooperative elects to purchase additional equipment.

2. Debt Capital

In addition to equity capital, cooperatives can also meet their financing needs through debt capital; that is, money from loans, bonds, or other financial instruments obtained through lenders or governmental programs. The extent to which debt capital must be used depends on the cooperative's line of business. For example, a small cooperative grocery store or automobile sharing business could potentially meet most of its capital needs from its members. In contrast, an electric or telephone cooperative is usually highly leveraged because of the intensive capital needs of the cooperative and the comparatively small resources of the members.

In many respects the sources and methods of debt financing of the cooperative are similar to those used by other types of businesses. As with other businesses, cooperatives incur short-term debt (usually defined as debt repayable in one year or less) for operating expenses, and so on and obtain long-term financing for fixed assets, capital improvements, and other large expenditures. To obtain financing, cooperatives, just like other businesses, must typically agree to various conditions, requirements, and restrictions in the financing documents, such as performance standards and debt-to-equity ratios.

Differences exist as well. For example, cooperatives have unique sources of financing available to them. Electric cooperatives and telecommunications cooperatives can receive lines of credit and long-term financing from the National Rural Utilities Cooperative Finance Corporation (CFC), which is owned by its members and provides a wide variety of other financial products. The U.S. Department of Agriculture's Rural Utilities Service makes direct loans and loan guarantees to electric cooperatives and telephone cooperatives. CoBank, a cooperative financial institution, provides loans and other financial services to agricultural cooperatives and electric cooperatives, among others. (CoBank is part of the Farm Credit System, which was created in the early 1900s by the U.S. Congress to provide credit to farmers and which is administered by the Farm Credit Administration.) The distinctive feature of CFC, CoBank, and other institutions that provide financing primarily for cooperatives is that they themselves are cooperatives, and can thus offer their cooperative members very competitive interest rates and prices on financial products, just as credit unions can offer competitive rates to their individual members.

Although financial programs for agricultural and electric cooperatives are well established, programs are also available from cooperative banks and federal, state and local governments to assist virtually any type and size of cooperative in obtaining financing, provided the cooperative can meet the applicable financial and organizational requirements. For example, loan or loan guarantee programs exist for water supply cooperatives, housing cooperatives, and broadband Internet cooperatives, among others. Because cooperatives often must meet certain requirements concerning voting rights, degree of business with nonmembers, amount of equity capital, and other matters typically addressed in the bylaws or organizational articles of the cooperative, financing and related matters must be considered before, rather than after, the formation of the cooperative.

Federated cooperatives, that is, cooperatives made up of other cooperatives, typically face different requirements in obtaining financing. Because federated cooperatives typically obtain all of their business from their member cooperatives, lenders seeking security are particularly interested in the agreements between federated cooperatives and their members. Not only are such member agreements part of the collateral pledged by the federated cooperative, but the loan agreement typically contains requirements and restrictions on any extension, termination, or assignment of such agreements. For that reason, federated cooperatives negotiating agreements with their members must include their lenders in the process as well, since lender approval will often be required pursuant to any mortgage, indenture or loan agreement. In practice, these considerations are taken into account when the federated cooperative is formed and its bylaws created.

C. Net Margins and Patronage Refunds

We will now explore some of the financial aspects of the cooperative that are least intuitive to those not familiar with the cooperative model. Before we discuss these aspects in detail and become familiar with the associated terminology, it might be helpful to examine these aspects in plain language, keeping in mind the origins and principles of cooperatives.

We know that cooperatives are often formed by persons or businesses that do not have the market power or capital to compete effectively on their own in their business sector. For that reason, as we have seen, members' initial capital contributions to the cooperative are usually small in comparison to the capital needs of the cooperative. Although cooperatives are not designed for the purpose of generating profits and dividends, but are instead meant to provide goods and services to their members at cost, cooperatives still need to increase equity capital over time for purposes of building reserves and meeting continuing capital needs. "At cost" operation indicates that any net margins of the cooperative would be returned to its members every year in proportion to their use of the cooperative's services. However, because the cooperative's members typically will not be in a position to make substantial capital contributions during the life of the cooperative, it makes sense that the cooperative can most easily increase equity capital by retaining part of the net margins that would ordinarily be returned to its members. Traditional cooperatives thus build up equity capital over time in a way that does not require large, one-time capital contributions from their members.

At this point, we should also consider that because some cooperatives provide goods and services to nonmembers as well as members, such cooperatives may also retain net margins that would otherwise be returned to nonmembers doing business with the cooperative. Thus nonmembers may contribute capital to the cooperative as well. We have referred to patrons as all persons, whether members or nonmembers, who do business with the cooperative. However, under the federal tax laws applicable to taxable cooperatives, the term *patron* has a distinct meaning: a patron is a person who does business with the cooperative and who is granted (typically through the bylaws or through contractual rights) the allocation of net margins. While we will focus on this definition of *patron* when discussing cooperative taxation in Chapter VII, to avoid confusion in the following discussion we will simply refer to "members," with the understanding that depending on the cooperative, nonmembers may be included as well.

Net margins. As mentioned in previous chapters, in the cooperative world, net earnings are typically referred to as "net margins." Because the purpose of the cooperative is to provide goods or services to its members at cost, rather than to generate a profit, in a perfect world there would be no net margins: prices paid by members would equal the cooperative's cost of goods and services and any operating costs and overhead of the cooperative. However, in addition to generating income sufficient to cover operating costs, cooperatives also must ensure that sufficient income is retained to meet future capital needs, as well as unexpected expenses. In any event, maintaining a perfect match between member prices and the cooperative's cost of goods and operating expenses would be impractical on a day-to-day basis. Accordingly, in accordance with prudent business practices, most cooperatives design their pricing so that net margins are generated each year.

Although the cooperative can retain a portion of net margins for the benefit of the cooperative as unallocated equity, typically most net margins are allocated to the members each year. These allocated net margins are commonly referred to as patronage refunds or capital credits. As the name implies, patronage refunds are allocated and distributed to members in proportion to their patronage of the cooperative; that is, their level of purchases of goods or services from the cooperative. The patronage refund is one of the key financial features of the cooperative, since it demonstrates not only the principle of "at cost" operation, but also the principle of proportionality of member benefits to members' use of the cooperative.

While cooperatives could make a full distribution of members' patronage refunds in cash each year, in practice the cooperative elects to retain some portion of patronage refunds for purposes of accumulating additional capital. The portion returned to members is typically called the cash patronage refund (also referred to as retired capital credits), while the portion retained by the cooperative is often called the retained patronage refund (also referred to as retained capital credits, the allocated capital retain, or allocated surplus). Retained patronage refunds are allocated to members' capital accounts as an additional equity investment of the members in the cooperative, and, as already discussed, provide an additional source of equity capital for the cooperative. Generally cooperatives retain the use of retained patronage refunds for a period of years before returning them to the members.

Retention of patronage refunds must be agreed to in writing between the members and the cooperative, and policies and procedures for retaining patronage refunds are typically set forth in the cooperative's bylaws. In the typical cooperative, the board of directors meets at the end of the year to determine what percentage of net margins will be allocated to the members as patronage refunds, and to determine what portion of the patronage refunds will be distributed to members. If the cooperative retains a portion of the patronage refund, the cooperative is required to provide written notice to each member each year of the amount allocated to each member's capital account. Such notices are referred to as written notices of allocation. Some cooperatives instead provide revolving capital certificates to their members that represent the portion of the patronage refund allocated to their capital account. Such revolving capital certificates typically do not bear interest.

Retained patronage refunds are either "qualified" or "nonqualified." The distinction is important primarily for tax purposes. For a retained patronage refund to be qualified, among other requirements, at least twenty percent of the total patronage refund must be paid in cash to the member, and the member must be provided the written notice of allocation (referred to as the "qualified written notice of allocation") within a specified period of time after the end of the cooperative's fiscal year. If qualified, the cooperative can claim a tax deduction for the retained patronage refund, and the amount of the retained patronage refund is treated as taxable income of the member. It thus follows that when the equity built up in the member's capital account through qualified retained patronage refunds is finally distributed to the member, there will be no taxable event for the member, since tax has already been paid.

If the patronage refund is nonqualified, it is not required to pay any portion of the refund to the member in cash in the year of distribution. In this case, the written notice of allocation provided to the member is referred to as the "nonqualified written notice of allocation." As one would expect, the cooperative cannot deduct the amount of nonqualified retained patronage refunds, and the amount of the retained patronage refund is not taxable to the member. However, when the equity built up in the member's capital account in this form is distributed to the member, the member will then recognize taxable income and the cooperative will be entitled to a tax deduction.

At this point, an example might be helpful in illustrating the connection between net margins, allocated and unallocated equity capital, and retained and cash patronage refunds. If ABC Cooperative enjoys net margins of $500,000 in a particular year, with $400,000 representing margins from transactions with patrons (members and nonmembers), then at the end of the year the patrons could potentially receive $400,000 in cash patronage refunds. ABC Cooperative's Board of Directors elects to retain $50,000 of the $400,000 in margins from patronage, and distribute the remaining $350,000 in the form of cash patronage refunds to patrons in proportion to their patronage with the cooperative. As a result, the $50,000 retained would be allocated equity capital representing additional patron equity in the cooperative, and would be allocated to patrons' capital accounts in proportion to their patronage.

While ABC Cooperative would receive a current tax deduction for the $350,000 in cash patronage refunds, to receive a current deduction for the retained $50,000 amount, the cooperative must distribute qualified written notices of allocation to the patrons stating each patron's allocation. Assuming the written notices are qualified, ABC Cooperative would receive a current deduction for the entire $400,000 in net margins generated by patrons.

We have now seen that the majority of the cooperative's equity comes not from the sale of stock or membership certificates, but through the cooperative's retention of a portion of the cooperative's net margins that would otherwise be returned to its members/users. In almost all cooperatives, this retention is part of a larger cycle in which retained equity is periodically returned to the cooperative's members through what are called equity redemption plans. Equity is thus "revolved" from the members, to the cooperative, and back to the members. We will discuss why this is the case, and how such equity redemption plans work, in the next section of this chapter.

D. Equity Redemption Plans

As discussed, retained patronage refunds are allocated to members' capital accounts with the understanding that such retained equity will be returned to the members at some point in time. If a cooperative's members receive cash patronage refunds each year, and the members indirectly benefit from the cooperative's use of retained equity, it may not be intuitive why it is important for the cooperative to return retained equity on a periodic basis, or for that matter, why the cooperative should return retained equity at all. The answer can be found in the cooperative principles.

Under cooperative principles, at all times, the ownership and control of the cooperative should be held by the current members of the cooperative. Also, members' equity in the cooperative should be proportionate to their current use of the cooperative. Although it would be preferable for every cooperative to be funded by its current members on the basis of their patronage, in practice this goal is difficult to attain. Since patronage refunds are based on the members' use of the cooperative, then it is clear that at any specific point in time each member is shouldering its appropriate share of responsibility for financing the cooperative, since retained equity is in proportion to use. Over time, however, as members' use of the cooperative changes, it is likely that an increasing portion of the cooperative's equity capital will be held by inactive members or members whose use of the cooperative has substantially decreased. To remedy this situation, it is desirable for the cooperative to have a system in place for periodically returning retained equity to its members. In this way, the ownership of the cooperative remains with its current users.

Of course there are practical reasons for establishing equity redemption programs as well. Although members of a cooperative likely expect that their cooperative will need to retain some amount of equity for the general use of the cooperative, members also expect that at some point in time the benefit of the postponed savings represented by retained equity will be returned to them. Also, members might prefer to receive a return of their equity investment upon retirement or at some other specified time. For all these reasons, cooperatives typically establish some method by which retained allocated equity is returned to the cooperative's members over time. For purposes of this chapter, we will refer to such a return as a redemption of allocated equity, or, more simply, equity redemption.

Although it is desirable for cooperatives to return allocated equity to their members, are cooperatives legally required to do so? To answer this question we would first look to the applicable state cooperative statute, assuming there is one, and any applicable federal tax laws. State cooperative statutes generally require that retained equity be returned to the members, although typically these statutes leave the method and timing to the discretion of the board of directors or to be set forth in the bylaws. Under some statutes the members can vote to give their cooperative the authority to permanently retain equity. In contrast, some cooperative statutes do not address the return of retained equity at all. As a further consideration, if a cooperative is organized under a state's general business corporation act or nonprofit corporation act, it is unlikely that such acts would address the return of retained equity, although the cooperative could address such matters in its bylaws.

Even if the applicable state statute does not expressly require that cooperatives return retained equity to the members, if the cooperative's board of directors consistently declined to do so, the courts examining the issue have indicated that members could bring an action against the board on the basis that the board's action is arbitrary and capricious and constitutes an abuse of discretion.[6] If the board of directors did decide to return retained equity, but did so in an inequitable manner, members could bring an action against the board on this basis as well. It is generally acknowledged that cooperatives have a general obligation to return retained equity to their members, and to establish a reasonable, fair equity redemption system. However, if the board of directors has a reasonable purpose in taking action regarding redemption of equity, the board will be protected by the business judgment rule.[7] In practice, actions by members alleging abuse of discretion in connection with equity redemption decisions have rarely succeeded.[8]

Some cooperatives are subject to additional rules and regulations governing return of retained equity by virtue of their participation in state and federal programs. For example, electric cooperatives with loans from or guaranteed by the USDA's Rural Utilities Service must obtain written approval in some circumstances before retiring capital credits (returning retained equity), or meet requirements set forth in the applicable federal regulations. Electric cooperatives that obtain power from the Tennessee Valley Authority (TVA) typically have restrictions on return of retained equity embedded in their contracts with TVA. Lenders, at least those familiar with cooperatives, may also place restrictions and requirements on a cooperative borrower's return of retained equity in the loan documents.

Now that we have discussed the broad discretion of the cooperative's board in connection with equity redemption, it is likely no surprise to learn that most courts have held that a member's right to the payment of retained patronage dividends vests upon the board's decision to redeem such equity, rather than upon allocation.[9] "Equity credits are not an indebtedness of a cooperative which is presently due and payable to the members, but represent an interest which will be paid to them at some unspecified later date to be determined by the board of directors."[10] For this reason, members do not have a breach of contract action against the cooperative for declining to redeem equity, although, as discussed, members might have a cause of action for breach of fiduciary duty if the board consistently refuses to redeem retained equity.

Although there are sound practical and legal reasons for having an equity redemption program, for those who find themselves advising a cooperative, be prepared to learn that the cooperative has no equity redemption program in place at all. Various surveys over the years have found that among certain types of cooperatives, such as agricultural marketing and supply cooperatives, a surprising percentage do in fact retain patronage refunds, but have no formal equity redemption program whatsoever. As a result, in these cooperatives an increasing percentage of equity is held by persons that no longer do business with the cooperative. Assuming that the cooperative has the financial resources available to return retained equity, for the reasons discussed above, it would be well advised to do so.

Assuming that a cooperative has an equity redemption program in place, such programs are typically classified as special equity redemption programs and systematic equity redemption programs. Special equity redemption programs return equity to members upon the occurrence of specified events, such as death or retirement. As one might guess, systematic equity redemption programs return equity to members on a periodic basis. In either case, the bylaws will specify how the plans operate. Let us first examine the two major types of systematic programs.

Revolving fund plan. Under this type of plan, the type most commonly used by cooperatives, retained patronage refunds are returned after a fixed period of years. If the period is fixed at twenty years, for example, a member who had equity retained by the cooperative in 1988 would actually have this equity redeemed in 2008. Equity is thus redeemed on a first-in, first-out basis.

In some cases the bylaws allow little deviation in equity redemption under such programs, and equity is redeemed on a fixed schedule, regardless of the cooperative's financial situation. In contrast, the bylaws of many cooperatives give the board of directors some discretion in operating the plan; for example, the board might have the ability to increase the number of years in the redemption cycle if the cooperative has an equity shortfall.

Base capital plan. This type of plan is designed to provide more accuracy in keeping members' equity investments proportional to their use of the cooperative. Each year, when the cooperative determines its equity capital needs for the coming year and considers patronage refunds, the cooperative distributes capital needs among the members in proportion to each member's use of the cooperative during a prior base period (usually three to ten years). If the member's use of the cooperative increased during the base period, or if the cooperative's equity requirements have increased, then the member might be deemed "under-invested." In this case, the cooperative will have the member add to his or her equity account by retaining a greater percentage of the member's patronage refund. In contrast, if a member's use of the cooperative has been decreasing, and the member is "over-invested," then the member might receive a greater percentage of the patronage refund in cash, or might even receive an additional redemption of equity payment.

Each of these plans has advantages and disadvantages. The revolving fund plan, while easy to understand and administer, does not precisely keep members' equity proportional to use. The base capital plan is quite accurate at keeping equity proportional to use, but is complex and can be difficult to administer.

In contrast to systematic programs, special equity redemption programs are triggered by specific events, such as death or retirement. Some programs redeem all of the member's equity when the event occurs; others instead redeem the equity over a set period of years. In the past, many cooperatives had only special equity redemption programs. Although many cooperatives have now adopted systematic programs, many continue to provide the special equity redemption programs as well.

Notes

1. Lambert v. Fisherman's Dock Coop., Inc., 280 A.2d 193, 197 (N.J. Super. Ct. App. Div. 1971).

2. Alaska Stat. § 10.15.130(a) (bylaws may authorize voting on basis of patronage); Fla. Stat. Ann. § 618.15(5) (same); N.Y. Coop. Corp. Law § 46 (same).

3. Vt. Stat. Ann. tit. 11, § 1001(9).

4. Md. Code Ann., Corps. and Ass'ns § 5-5A-20 (voting rights of members in federated consumer cooperative not required to be on one-member, one-vote basis, provided voting may not be based solely on amount of investment by a member or on membership capital attributable to member).

5. Fla. Stat. Ann. § 618.15.

6. *See* Lake Region Packing Ass'n, Inc. v. Furze, 327 So.2d 212 (Fla. 1976) (judicial review of cooperative's refusal to redeem is available if directors' refusal to do so constitutes abuse of discretion, breach of trust, or is based on fraud, illegality or inequity).

7. *See, e.g.*, Great Rivers Co-op. of Southeastern Iowa v. Farmland Indus., Inc., 198 F.3d 685 (8th Cir. 1999).

8. *See* Ga. Turkey Farms, Inc. v. Hardigree, 369 S.E.2d 803 (Ga. App. 1988); Claassen v. Farmers Grain Co-op., 490 P.2d 376 (Kan. 1971) (where bylaws did not provide for mandatory payment of retained equity upon member's death, cooperative was not required to make provision for immediate payment of retained equity to member's estate).

9. *See* In re FCX, Inc., 853 F.2d 1149 (4th Cir. 1988); Atchison County Farmers Union Coop. Ass'n v. Turnbull, 736 P.2d 917 (Kan. 1987); Howard v. Eatonton Coop. Feed Co., 177 S.E.2d 658 (Ga. 1970). *See also* In re Greensboro Lumber Co., 157 B.R. 921 (Bankr. M.D. Ga. 1993).

10. *Howard*, 177 S.E.2d at 662.

Further Reading

Cooperative Financing and Taxation: Farmer Cooperatives in the United States, USDA COOPERATIVE INFORMATION REPORT No. 1, Section 9 (1995).

Managing Your Cooperative's Equity, USDA COOPERATIVE INFORMATION REPORT No. 56 (1997).

Robert C. Rathbone & Roger A. Wissman, *Equity Redemption and Member Equity Allocation Practices of Agricultural Cooperatives*, USDA AGRICULTURE RESEARCH SERVICE RESEARCH REPORT No. 124 (1993).

VII

Taxation of Cooperatives

We have already discussed many of the unique characteristics of the cooperative that differentiate it from other types of business entities. Taxation is yet another such characteristic, and an entire body of federal tax law has developed involving the cooperative form of business. As with any other form of corporate entity, it is imperative that one considering the use of the cooperative form or advising a cooperative have at least a basic understanding of the of tax law governing that form of business.

The purpose of this chapter is to provide an overview of the federal income tax laws relating to the cooperative form of business. We have not attempted in this chapter to address those aspects of federal tax equally applicable to cooperatives and other forms of organization. Likewise, we have not attempted to provide a survey of state tax issues applicable to cooperatives. Rather, we have confined this discussion to the central questions involving federal income tax law dealing with cooperatives.

One must consider five central questions concerning the taxation of cooperatives: (1) What is a cooperative for federal tax purposes; (2) is the cooperative a taxable entity; (3) if the cooperative is a taxable entity, how is the cooperative taxed; (4) how are the members or patrons of the cooperative taxed; and (5) how does a cooperative obtain tax-exempt status and how must it operate to retain such status? Each of these questions will be addressed in this chapter.

A. What Is a Cooperative for Federal Tax Purposes?

Many states have enacted specific statues that authorize the creation and operation of cooperatives or that permit other types of organizations to operate on a cooperative basis. To determine whether such organizations satisfy each state's cooperative organizational statute, and what legal rights exist between the cooperative and its patrons or members, the applicable state law must be consulted. However, to determine whether an organization operates on a cooperative basis for federal tax purposes, one must look to federal law. Federal tax law sources include the Internal Revenue Code (IRC), the Department of the Treasury's regulations, federal tax cases, and certain guidance from the Internal Revenue Service (IRS).[1]

The Code does not define "cooperative," "operating on a cooperative basis,"[2] or "organized and operated on a cooperative basis."[3] Instead, case law and IRS guidance have historically provided the determining criteria. The seminal case on cooperative operation is *Puget Sound Plywood, Inc. v. C.I.R.*[4] In that case, the Tax Court considered whether a workers cooperative association organized under state law was operated on a cooperative basis, and thus could deduct patronage dividends. In deciding this issue, the Court cited three primary factors of cooperative operation:

(1) Subordination of capital;
(2) Democratic control by members; and
(3) Vesting in and allocation among members of the excess of operating revenues over costs.

The first principle, "subordination of capital," entails placing the control and direction of the organization in the members. Furthermore, the members should receive the pecuniary benefits attributable to the organization's operation rather than having those pecuniary benefits go to capital contributors. The second principle requires the cooperative to hold meetings at which members may vote on a one-member/one-vote basis. Under the third principle, a cooperative must allocate and distribute its net earnings, as opposed to reinvesting such earnings to generate profits. The third principle is occasionally bifurcated by creating a fourth principle known as the "operation at cost" principle.

The Code sections applicable to different types of cooperatives may impose additional requirements in addition to these basic cooperative principles. Any requirements in addition to the *Puget Sound* cooperative principles are discussed in the relevant section below. However, most types of cooperatives must satisfy, at a minimum, the basic cooperative principles of *Puget Sound*.[5]

B. Is the Cooperative a Taxable Entity?[6]

In this section, we will discuss whether a cooperative is a taxable entity, as opposed to being completely disregarded for tax purposes. For purposes of this section, "taxable entity" does not refer to whether an organization is tax exempt. Instead, it refers to an entity that is subject to the federal tax laws as an entity that is separate from its owners.[7]

Is the Cooperative a Taxable Entity? 89

Federal tax law generally treats an entity as either a taxable entity (e.g., corporation or partnership) or as simply disregarded for federal tax purposes. For example, a corporation is a separate taxpayer, while a sole proprietorship is disregarded as an entity that is separate from its owner. Disregarded entities generally have little or no reporting obligations to the IRS and do not separately pay federal income taxes.

Federal law governs whether an entity is a taxable entity or is simply disregarded for federal tax purposes. Under federal law, however, the state law authorizing the entity's form of organization plays an important role in determining whether a cooperative is a taxable entity, and how the cooperative is ultimately taxed.[8] Thus, cooperatives may or may not be taxable entities, depending on the interplay between federal tax laws and relevant state laws.[9]

The federal tax rules governing whether an entity is a taxable entity are called "check-the-box" regulations.[10] If an entity is considered a taxable entity, these regulations further classify the entity to determine whether it is taxed as a corporation or partnership. An entity's classification depends upon whether it has one or more owners.[11] If the entity has only one owner, it must be classified as either a disregarded entity or a corporation.[12] If the entity has more than one owner, it must be classified as a corporation or a partnership.[13]

Under the check-the-box regulations, only an "eligible entity" may choose its tax classification for federal tax purposes.[14] An eligible entity is a "business entity" that is not subject to mandatory classification as a corporation (commonly referred to as a "per se corporation") or other special classification.[15] A business entity is defined as any entity recognized for federal tax purposes (including a disregarded entity) that is not a trust or subject to special classification under the Code.[16] Per se corporations generally include state law corporations and other entities similar to corporations, or entities that receive special treatment under the Code.[17]

Now that we have addressed the general rules of entity classification, the next question is whether a cooperative is a taxable entity?[18] The answer to this question depends on (1) whether the cooperative is a per se corporation or an eligible entity and (2) if the cooperative is an eligible entity, whether the cooperative elects corporate, partnership, or disregarded classification.

Most cooperatives are taxable entities because they are classified as per se corporations. They receive mandatory classification as a corporation because either they were formed under a state's corporation statute or the state cooperative statute refers to such cooperatives as corporations.[19] Further, most cooperatives cannot elect to be disregarded as a taxable entity because, by nature, cooperatives have multiple owners.

The issue of whether a cooperative may receive partnership treatment (i.e., flow-through tax treatment) is an interesting one because most cooperatives, if subject to Subchapter T, may receive similar treatment by way of a deduction for patronage dividends.[20] In other words, most nonexempt cooperatives may take a deduction for patronage net earnings they distribute in accordance with Subchapter T. As a result, similar to partnerships, deductible distributions of a Subchapter T cooperative's earnings are taxed only at the patron- or member-level.[21]

Nonetheless, some cooperatives have elected tax classification as a partnership.[22] Such cooperatives have probably elected partnership classification due to the restrictions of Subchapter T. As explained later in this chapter, Subchapter T imposes certain restrictions on the deductibility of patronage dividends. Such restrictions relate to the timing of distributions, form of distributions, method of allocating distributions among patrons, and limitations on the source of income.

As discussed in Chapter II, some states have recently created organizational statutes authorizing the formation of cooperatives that have certain characteristics of limited liability companies, referred to in this book as limited cooperative associations. In Private Letter Ruling 200139020, the IRS considered whether such a cooperative was an eligible entity or a per se corporation.[23] The IRS studied the state's Cooperative Limited Liability Company Act, noting among other things that the statute did not define the cooperative as a corporation. The IRS ultimately concluded that the cooperative was not a per se corporation, and was therefore an eligible entity under the check-the-box regulations.

C. If the Cooperative Is a Taxable Entity, How Is the Cooperative Taxed?

If a cooperative is a separate taxable entity for federal tax purposes, the next logical question is how it will pay tax. There are two basic systems of tax treatment of cooperatives. The first system incorporates the basic taxation of regular Subchapter C corporations and applies special deductions[24] or other tax benefits to accommodate the unique nature of cooperative operation. The second system of taxation is an outright exemption from tax. Both systems of taxation recognize the nonprofit nature of cooperatives, and both recognize the inequity of double taxation on a cooperative's income. However, it is important to remember that no cooperative is entirely immune from taxation.

D. Regular Corporate Taxation With Special Benefits to Cooperatives

Unless a cooperative is tax exempt or classified as a partnership, the rules and rates of regular corporate[25] taxation apply. Thus, the starting point for cooperative taxation is the rules applicable to Subchapter C corporations.[26] From that point, the next step is to review the special tax benefits applicable to each type of cooperative. The two most common types of cooperatives subject to regular corporate tax are (1) Subchapter T cooperatives and (2) Section 521 farmers' cooperatives.[27]

1. Subchapter T Cooperatives

In the context of taxation, when most persons refer to cooperatives, they typically are referring to Subchapter T cooperatives. These cooperatives are called "Subchapter T cooperatives" because the rules providing special tax treatment to such cooperatives are located in Subchapter T of the Code. So many cooperatives are subject to Subchapter T because it encompasses any corporation operating on a cooperative basis.[28]

Subchapter T provides two types of tax benefits: (1) special deductions and (2) a special computation of tax in years when the cooperative has insufficient taxable income to take certain special deductions.

a. Applicability of Subchapter T

Subchapter T applies to (1) Section 521 farmers' cooperatives; and (2) any corporation operating on a cooperative basis. However, it excludes (1) tax-exempt organizations (except Section 521 farmers' cooperatives);[29] (2) mutual savings banks, cooperative banks, and domestic building and loan associations under Subchapter H, Part II; (3) Subchapter L insurance companies;[30] and (4) rural electric cooperatives and rural telephone cooperatives.

b. Special Deductions

The primary tax benefit of Subchapter T is the special deduction[31] for certain returns or allocations of earnings to patrons. These special deductions can be categorized into two types: (1) deductions *used to compute* gross income and (2) deductions *from* gross income. Additionally, some of these special deductions apply to all cooperatives, and some apply exclusively to Section 521 farmers' cooperatives.

All Subchapter T cooperatives may reduce taxable income with deductions for the following items, subject to restrictions discussed in detail:

(1) patronage dividends paid as money, other property, or qualified written notices of allocation;
(2) redemption of nonqualified written notices of allocation paid as patronage dividends;

(3) per-unit retain allocations; and
(4) redemption of nonqualified per-unit retain certificates.

The rules governing special deductions can be complex and often confusing. Therefore, in reviewing the rules for each special deduction, we must consider four primary issues with respect to each special deduction:

(1) In what form must the transfer or distribution to patrons occur?
(2) When must the transfer or distribution to patrons occur?
(3) When must the underlying patronage business (or marketing) occur?
(4) Which earnings can generate special deductions?

The first two types of special deductions give rise to deductions *from* gross income.[32] The latter two types give rise to deductions used *to compute* gross income. The distinction is important for those tax rules that depend on the amount of a taxpayer's gross income.[33]

Section 521 farmers' cooperatives receive additional special deductions that are unavailable to other Subchapter T cooperatives. In addition to the distributions that are deductible by all Subchapter T cooperatives, Section 521 farmers' cooperatives may deduct the following: (1) certain dividends paid on capital stock or other similar interests; (2) certain payments based on patronage from non-patronage and U.S. government sources (i.e., the U.S. government and any of its agencies), and (3) redemptions of nonqualified written notices of allocation from non-patronage or U.S. government sources.[34]

c. Definitions Applicable to Subchapter T

Subchapter T provides a great benefit to cooperatives in the form of special deductions and modified tax calculation. To avoid any manipulation of such benefits, Congress imposed restrictive rules and created complex definitions. Thus, before any meaningful discussion of Subchapter T can occur, one should establish the definitions of common Subchapter T terms.

i. Patronage Earnings and Losses

A fundamental concept in Subchapter T is "patronage earnings." Patronage earnings (and losses) are earnings (and losses) derived from business done with or for patrons ("patronage business") of the cooperative.[35] In determining the net earnings of a cooperative, the cooperative may offset patronage losses from one allocation unit against patronage earnings of another allocation unit.[36] An allocation unit may include any functional, divisional, departmental, geographic, or other category of allocating net earnings.[37] Before the cooperative may employ the netting options, it must provide notice to its members.[38]

Regular Corporate Taxation With Special Benefits to Cooperatives 93

ii. Patronage Dividends

Patronage dividends are a common form of Subchapter T tax benefits. The term "patronage dividend" refers to an amount distributed to patrons that meets three criteria: (a) The amount is determined with reference to the net earnings of the cooperative from patronage business, (b) its amount must be computed on the basis of patronage business with or for each patron, measured by value or quantity, and (c) the cooperative had a binding obligation to distribute such amount before the cooperative itself received the amount.[39]

The first two criteria concern the computation and source of the patronage dividend. The first criterion requires the payment or transfer to be computed with respect to the "net earnings" of patronage business.[40] In other words, to compute a patronage dividend, the cooperative must first compute the amount of patronage-sourced net earnings.[41]

To compute the amount of a patronage dividend, the first step[42] is to compute the net earnings of the cooperative. For the purpose of computing a patronage dividend, "net earnings" means the "excess of amounts retained (or assessed) by the organization to cover expenses or other items over the amount of such expenses or other items."[43] The cooperative will compute net earnings by taking a reduction for dividends paid on capital stock or other proprietary capital interests;[44] however, no such reduction is made to the extent the cooperative is bound to pay such dividends on capital interests in addition to amounts otherwise payable to patrons.[45] There is no decrease for federal income taxes.[46]

Before the American Jobs Creation Act of 2004, cooperatives were required to reduce net earnings by capital stock dividends,[47] allocating such amounts against patronage and non-patronage earnings. This rule usually resulted in lower patronage net earnings, and thus lower patronage dividends. In accordance with the trend in cooperative evolution, Congress believed that Subchapter T cooperatives should be permitted to issue capital stock dividends, and to pay dividends on such stock, without negatively impacting their potential patronage dividends.[48] As a result, the Code was amended in 2004[49] to allow Subchapter T cooperatives to issue certain capital stock dividends without reducing their patronage net earnings (and without reducing their potential for patronage dividends).[50]

After the cooperative computes its net earnings, it must compute the portion of such net earnings which was generated by patronage business (i.e., attributable to patronage-source income). Patronage-sourced income refers to income generated by a transaction that facilitates the cooperative's marketing,[51] purchasing, or service activity.[52] It does not include income generated to "enhance the profitability of the cooperative as a whole."[53]

When the cooperative computes net earnings from patronage business, it can then determine the amount of its net earnings which gives rise to a patronage dividend deduction. Note that the cooperative need not distribute all net earnings to patrons; it may decide to keep some to cover expected future expenses. If the cooperative keeps such amounts, it will not receive a deduction in the current taxable year for such amounts.

The second criterion to qualify as a patronage dividend requires the cooperative to compute each patron's distribution on a patronage basis. In other words, each patron's patronage dividend is calculated based on the amount of patronage business generated by (or attributable to) such patron. The amount of patronage business can be based on quantity or value of each patron's patronage business.[54]

Finally, the third criterion requires the cooperative to make patronage dividends pursuant to a preexisting obligation.[55] The regulations require the preexisting obligation to be a valid, written obligation that is enforceable under state law or pursuant to the provisions of the bylaws, articles, or other written contract.[56] The cooperative must have incurred the obligation before the cooperative received the amount it paid to the patron.[57]

A few items are expressly excluded from the definition of patronage dividends. These include amounts that represent (a) earnings from non-patronage business and (b) earnings from business done with patrons to whom the cooperative does not distribute any amount or to whom the cooperative distributes smaller amounts than given to other patrons on substantially similar transactions.[58] For example, if a cooperative does not make dividends to nonmember patrons, it may not take a deduction for the portion of patronage dividends generated by nonmember business, even if such dividends are paid to members/patrons.[59]

Patronage dividends do not include redemptions of capital stock, redemption or satisfaction of certificates of indebtedness, revolving fund certificates, retain certificates, letters of advice, or other similar documents, even if such documents were originally paid as patronage dividends.[60] Also excluded is any amount paid to the extent such amount is fixed without reference to the net earnings of the cooperative from patronage business.[61]

iii. Written Notice of Allocation (Qualified and Nonqualified)

Written notices of allocation are another important component of Subchapter T's tax benefits. Written notices of allocation provide notice to a patron of the amount to which such patron is entitled without requiring the cooperative to immediately distribute such allocation in cash or property.

Written notices of allocation include notices which disclose to the patron (a) the stated dollar amount allocated to such patron and (b) any portion thereof that constitutes a patronage dividend.[62] The portion constituting a patronage dividend may be expressed as a dollar amount or as a percentage of the written notice of allocation.[63] Written notices of allocation may include any fund certificate, retain certificate, certificate of indebtedness, letter of advice, or other written notice.[64]

There are two types of written notices of allocation: qualified and nonqualified. The primary distinction between the two is the timing of their related deduction by the cooperative. Qualified written notices are deductible upon distribution;[65] nonqualified written notices are deductible, if at all, when actually redeemed.[66]

A qualified written notice of allocation includes any written notice of allocation that satisfies either of the following: (a) The written notice of allocation is redeemable in cash at its stated dollar amount at any time within the period beginning on the date of such written notice of allocation is distributed and ending not earlier than ninety days from that date[67] or (b) the recipient must consent to account for the written notice of allocation's stated dollar amount in the recipient's taxable income.[68] In addition, to qualify for treatment as a patronage dividend or a Section 1382(c)(2)(A) allocation, twenty percent or more of the amount of the patronage dividend must be paid in cash or qualified check.[69]

A recipient provides consent to account for the written notice of allocation as taxable income by doing any of the following: (1) providing consent in writing, (2) if the bylaws provide membership constitutes such consent, obtaining membership in the cooperative and receiving a written notification of such bylaw policy, or (3) only if neither of the prior two options apply, endorsing and cashing a qualified check on or before the ninetieth day after the close of the payment period of the taxable year in which the payment is made.[70]

Nonqualified written notices of allocation include all written notices of allocation that are not deemed qualified.[71]

iv. Per-Unit Retain Allocation and Certificate

A per-unit retain allocation includes any allocation to a patron with respect to products marketed for such patron, and only if such allocation was determined without reference to the net earnings of the cooperative and pursuant to an agreement between the cooperative and the patron.[72] Likewise, a per-unit retain certificate includes any written notice which discloses to the patron the stated dollar amount of the patron's per-unit retain allocation.[73]

A per-unit retain certificate becomes qualified only when the distributee has agreed to include the amount stated on the certificate in the distributee's gross income.[74] The required agreement is satisfied when it is evidenced in writing or by obtaining or retaining membership in the cooperative, but only if the cooperative has a bylaw provision stating that membership in the cooperative constitutes such an agreement and the distributee has received a copy or notice of such provision.[75] A nonqualified per-unit retain certificate includes any per-unit retain certificate that is not qualified.[76]

d. Types of Special Deductions

i. Special Deductions for Patronage Dividends Paid as Money, Property, or Qualified Written Notices of Allocation

For a cooperative to receive a deduction for distributing patronage dividends, Subchapter T requires more than just allocating earnings among the patrons' capital accounts. The deduction is permitted only to the extent a patronage dividend is paid to patrons as (1) money; (2) qualified written notices of allocation; or (3) other property except nonqualified written notices of allocation.[77] The patronage dividend also must have been paid (1) during the payment period[78] and (2) with respect to patronage occurring during the taxable year of the payment period.[79]

ii. Special Deductions for Redemption of Nonqualified Written Notices of Allocation

Subchapter T also provides a special deduction for redemption of nonqualified written notices of allocation, but only when such redemption satisfies certain rules. First, it must have been paid as (1) money, or (2) other property except another written notice of allocation.[80] Second, the underlying nonqualified written notice of allocation (not the actual redemption) must have been distributed as a patronage dividend during the payment period for the taxable year in which the patronage occurred.[81]

The regulations provide additional guidance on ancillary issues for redemptions of nonqualified written notices of allocation. If the redemption occurs during the payment period of two or more taxable years,[82] then the cooperative may take the deduction only in the earlier tax year.[83] The deduction cannot exceed the stated dollar amount on the written notice of allocation.[84] When the cooperative transfers property in redemption of the nonqualified written notice of allocation, the deductible amount shall be the property's fair market value, but not more than the stated value of the nonqualified written notice of allocation.[85] Additionally, when the redemption exceeds the stated dollar amount of the nonqualified written notice of allocation, such excess is treated under other applicable provisions of the Code, such as Section 163 (regarding deductions for interest payments) for example.[86]

iii. Special Deductions for Per-Unit Retain Allocations

The third special deduction relates to per-unit retain allocations. A per unit retain allocation is an allocation made to patrons with respect to products marketed for such patrons, where the allocation is calculated without reference to the net earnings of the cooperative.[87] Subchapter T permits a deduction for per-unit retain allocations for products marketed during a taxable year,[88] and only to the extent paid in the payment period of such taxable year as (1) money, (2) qualified per-unit retain certificates, or (3) other property (except nonqualified per unit retain certificates).[89]

iv. Special Deductions for Redemption of Nonqualified Per-Unit Retain Certificates

The final special deduction available to all Subchapter T cooperatives is for payments in redemption of nonqualified per-unit retain certificates. The redemption payment must consist of money or other property, except another per-unit retain certificate.[90] The underlying nonqualified per-unit retain certificate (not the actual redemption) must have been paid during the payment period for the taxable year during which the marketing occurred.[91]

v. Special Deductions for Section 521 Farmers' Cooperatives—Dividends on Capital Stock

Although Subchapter T imposes regular corporate taxation on Section 521 farmers' cooperatives, which are otherwise considered tax exempt, it also provides special deductions not available to other Subchapter T cooperatives.[92] The first of these permits a deduction for dividends paid on capital stock.[93] For purposes of this deduction, "capital stock" refers to any voting or nonvoting common stock, preferred stock, or any other form of capital interest represented by capital retain certificates, revolving fund certificates, letters of advice, or other evidence of proprietary interest in a cooperative.[94]

Section 521 farmers' cooperatives may take a deduction for dividends paid on capital stock only in the tax year the dividend was actually or constructively paid.[95] The regulations also establish the presumption that when a check is mailed in an envelope that is properly addressed, the dividend check is presumed paid in the taxable year in which it would ordinarily be received through the mail, regardless of whether the shareholder actually receives the check at that time.[96] Lastly, the accounting basis or method of a cooperative is immaterial in determining when a dividend payment is paid to a capital stock shareholder.[97]

vi. Special Deductions for Section 521 Farmers' Cooperatives—Distributions from Non-Patronage Earnings and U.S. Government Sources

Section 521 farmers' cooperatives may also deduct payments made to patrons with respect to earnings derived from (1) non-patronage sources and (2) business done with the U.S. government.[98] The payment (not the underlying notice of allocation) must have been made during the relevant tax year's payment period, and must have been made in money, qualified written notices of allocation, or other property (except nonqualified written notices of allocation).[99]

The regulations provide guidance on timing and valuation of the deduction, and most importantly, on determining whether earnings are derived from non-patronage sources. Non-patronage-sourced income includes income that is incidental and derived from sources that are not directly related to marketing, purchasing, or service activities of the cooperative.[100]

In allocating net earnings (whether patronage or non-patronage sourced), a cooperative must determine the amount of patronage business done with each patron. However, a computational issue arises when a cooperative generates earnings throughout multiple years, or recognizes gain which was built up during multiple years, which are allocable to patrons who may or may not remain patrons throughout all of such years. In other words, how should a cooperative with constantly changing patrons allocate earnings generated during multiple years? In this situation, the cooperative should allocate earnings among patrons only for years in which the patrons were actually patrons.[101] For example, to allocate a net gain from the sale of a capital asset held by the cooperative for many years (normally non-patronage earnings), the cooperative must allocate the net gain among patrons on the basis of patronage business done with each patron. To the extent possible, the allocation should spread the net gain among each year the cooperative owned the capital asset. If persons were patrons for only selected years, they would receive allocation from the net gain for only those particular years (determined with respect to their patronage business during those years).[102]

The following rules relate to determining the timing and amount of payments to patrons. A payment is deemed paid in money if paid by qualified check that was issued during the payment period and is endorsed and cashed on or before the ninetieth day after the close of such payment period.[103] If a payment is made as a qualified written notice of allocation, then the amount is deemed paid when the qualified written notice of allocation is issued to the patron.[104] The deductible amount of any qualified written notice of allocation is its stated dollar amount.[105]

vii. Special Deductions for Section 521 Farmers' Cooperatives—Redemptions Related to Non-Patronage Sources and U.S. Government Sources

The final deduction for Section 521 farmers' cooperatives relates to redemptions of nonqualified written notices of allocation. The deduction for Section 521 farmers cooperative is similar to the deduction for all Subchapter T cooperatives, except for one difference: the written notice of allocation may relate to earnings derived from business done with non-patronage sources or U.S. government sources.[106]

The redemption must take the form of money or other property except written notices of allocation. The written notice of allocation must have been paid to the patron on a patronage basis during the payment period for the taxable year in which the earnings were derived.[107] The deduction is limited to the stated amount on the nonqualified written notice of allocation;[108] however, any excess payment may qualify for an interest deduction under Section 163.[109]

e. *Timing Rules for Special Deductions*

As a Subchapter T cooperative's fiscal year ends, the cooperative usually closes its books and should distribute any patronage dividends to its patrons. Congress recognized, however, that cooperatives cannot perform this task immediately, especially when the cooperative has many patrons. Therefore, Subchapter T permits the cooperative to issue certain distributions during an extended "payment period." A payment period starts on the first day of the tax year and extends to the fifteenth day of the ninth month after the close of the cooperative's taxable year.[110]

Two additional timing rules exclusive to Subchapter T cooperatives apply to qualified checks and written notices of allocation. The cooperative may treat a payment by "qualified check" as a payment of money during the payment period if (1) the qualified check is paid within the payment period and (2) the check is endorsed and cashed within ninety days after the close of the payment period.[111] So, as long as the patron cashes the check within ninety days after the payment period, the cooperative can still take a deduction during the prior taxable year, assuming the transfer satisfies other applicable rules of Subchapter T. A qualified check is an instrument paid to a patron and on which a notice is printed that the endorsement and cashing of such instrument constitutes the patron's consent to include the stated dollar amount in the patron's taxable income.[112] As for written notices of allocation, they are deemed paid when issued to a patron.

To determine when a cooperative must make distributions of patronage dividends, it must determine the year in which the corresponding patronage business occurred. Two other timing rules assist Subchapter T cooperatives in making this determination. The first patronage timing rule involves pooling arrangements for marketing products. Under such an arrangement, patronage is deemed to occur during the taxable year in which the pool closes.[113] When the pool closes is a facts and circumstances test; however, the practices and operations of the cooperative control the determination.[114] When the cooperative distributes retain allocations, the related marketing is deemed to occur during any taxable year that the pool is open.[115]

The second patronage timing rule applies when any portion of patronage earnings is included in a cooperative's gross income in a taxable year after which the patronage earnings occurred. When such a delay occurs, for any patronage dividend or redemption of a nonqualified written notice of allocation paid as a patronage dividend, the patronage is deemed to occur during the taxable year when the cooperative includes the patronage earnings in its gross income.[116] For example, this rule has been applied where a cooperative received a qualified per unit retain certificate from its patron, which was also a cooperative, in a year after it purchased grain from the patron.[117] In this situation, even though the actual patronage transaction occurred in the previous year, because the income was not recognized by the cooperative until the subsequent year, the patronage was deemed to occur in the subsequent year.

f. Special Tax Computation of Subchapter T Cooperatives

A special deduction provides no current benefit to a cooperative when the cooperative has no current taxable income to reduce. To ensure Subchapter T cooperatives currently receive the benefit of certain patronage deductions (redemptions of previously distributed notices and certificates), Subchapter T provides for a modified calculation of taxes, usually resulting in a tax credit or refund.[118]

Take the following example:[119] Cooperative X generated earnings from business with patrons in Year 1 and distributed a nonqualified written notice of allocation to patrons related to such earnings during the payment period of Year 1. Also in Year 1, Cooperative X paid tax on the patronage earnings. Because the written notice of allocation was nonqualified, Cooperative X took no deduction in Year 1. During the payment period of Year 2, Cooperative X redeemed the previously-issued nonqualified written notices of allocation in cash. In Year 2, Cooperative X would have taken a deduction, but assume it generated a loss for Year 2. But for a special rule, Cooperative X would receive no benefit from the deduction in Year 2.

Under Subchapter T's modified tax computation rule, if (a) the cooperative redeems nonqualified written notices of allocation[120] or nonqualified per-unit retain certificates[121] (collectively "nonqualified notices") and (b) the modified tax calculation results in a lower tax burden, then the modified tax calculation must be used.[122] The modified tax method reclassifies the prior issued *nonqualified* notice as a *qualified* written notice of allocation or a qualified per-unit retain certificate (collectively "qualified notices"). Reclassifying nonqualified notices as qualified notices results in a hypothetical deduction in the tax year of the payment period such nonqualified notice was paid.[123]

The modified tax generally results in a decrease in the current year's tax.[124] The amount of such decrease equals any decrease in the current year and any prior year's tax resulting from reclassifying the relevant nonqualified notice as a qualified notice.[125] In determining the decrease of tax in the current year or any prior year resulting from the reclassification, the relevant tax years include any year the tax of which is affected by the reclassification.[126] Additionally, the decrease in any prior taxable year's tax equals the difference between:

> (1) the amount shown on the affected prior year's tax return, plus any previously assessed (or collected) deficiencies, and less any previous rebates, and

(2) the affected prior year's tax recomputed with the reclassification, including any adjustments to items dependent on gross income.[127]

The benefits of the modified tax computation may include a reduction in tax. Additionally, if the aggregate reduction in tax exceeds the tax for the current year, then the cooperative may treat the excess as an overpayment of estimated tax on the last day of the taxable year.[128] As such, the cooperative may claim a refund or tax credit for the deemed overpayment.

If the modified method results in lesser tax, then the cooperative may not take the otherwise permitted deduction for redemption of the nonqualified notice.[129] If the modified method results in the same amount of tax as the normal method, the Subchapter T treats the tax as if it were computed under the normal method.[130] The prior year's hypothetical deductions resulting from reclassifying nonqualified notices as qualified notices only assist in computing the reduction in current year tax.[131]

g. Taxation of Subchapter T Patrons

No discussion of Subchapter T is complete without addressing the taxation of Subchapter T patrons. Subchapter T clarifies the pre-Subchapter T confusion surrounding when patrons should include allocations and distributions from cooperatives in their taxable income.

As a general rule, patrons must adhere to the rule regarding recognition of taxable income.[132] This rule seems to require taxation of anything that resembles income. The general rule, however, yields to the more specific rules under Subchapter T.[133] The regulations under the general rule provide rules specifically related to amounts received from cooperatives, unless the treatment of a particular item is governed by Subchapter T.[134]

Patrons must include in their taxable income in the tax year received any money, qualified written notice of allocation, or other property except nonqualified written notices of allocation when such amounts are paid as (1) a patronage dividend or (2) a distribution from a Section 521 farmers' cooperative on a patronage basis and out of the earnings derived from nonpatronage or U.S. government sources.[135] Patrons must also include as gross income any per-unit retain allocation paid as a qualified per-unit retain certificate in the taxable year received.[136]

Additionally, patrons must include the gain from sale or other disposition of nonqualified notices[137] paid as patronage dividends or by a Section 521 farmers' cooperative as earnings from non-patronage or U.S. government sources.[138] The taxable gain equals the excess of the stated dollar amount of the nonqualified notice over the patron's basis in the nonqualified notice.[139] Any resulting taxable gain is generally deemed ordinary income.[140] In addition, if the patron receives an amount realized from the sale or other disposition of the nonqualified notice any amount in excess of the stated dollar amount on the nonqualified notice, such excess is taxed as interest, or under other applicable sections of the Code.[141]

A patron's basis in a nonqualified notice depends upon from whom the patron received the nonqualified notice. If a patron received the nonqualified notice from the payor-cooperative, the patron's basis therein is zero.[142] If the patron received the nonqualified notice from a decedent, the patron receives a carry-over basis, or the basis which decedent held in the nonqualified notice.[143]

Subchapter T also provides exclusions from gross income for two items of otherwise taxable income.[144] Patrons may exclude certain patronage dividends or amounts received in redemption, sale, or other disposition of nonqualified written notices of allocation paid as a patronage dividend to the extent such payments are (1) taken into account as an adjustment to basis of property[145] or (2) attributable to personal, living, or family items.[146] The regulations under Subchapter T clarify that distributions attributable to personal, living, or family items relate to purchases of supplies, equipment, or services which were not used in the trade or business and the cost of which was not deductible under § 212. In addition, amounts properly taken into account as adjustments to basis include amounts received with respect to the marketing or purchasing of a capital asset[147] or depreciable property used in a trade or business.[148]

The regulations also explain how payments are taken into account as an adjustment to the basis of property.[149] In the first example, a farmer-patron purchases an implement, to be used in the farmer's business, from a cooperative. At that time, the farmer-patron would presumably receive a cost basis in the implement.[150] Subsequently, the cooperative distributes a deductible patronage dividend with respect to this transaction to the farmer-patron. As a result of the patronage dividend, the farmer-patron will adjust downward the basis of the implement by the amount received.

2. Section 521 Farmers' Cooperatives

Congress has long felt farmers' cooperatives should receive special tax treatment. As a result, the federal tax law has continuously provided tax benefits, including exemption, to farmers' cooperatives.[151] In 1962, it added Subchapter T, which applies to Section 521 farmers' cooperatives and subjects them to regular corporate taxation.[152]

The Code actually labels Section 521 farmers' cooperatives as tax exempt.[153] However, according to Subchapter T, they are treated similar to other Subchapter T cooperatives, except for the additional tax benefits exclusive to Section 521 farmers' cooperatives.[154] In other words, they are subject to income tax but receive additional tax benefits. Thus, for purposes of this chapter, Section 521 farmers' cooperatives are categorized as taxable Subchapter T cooperatives.[155]

a. Applicability of Section 521

Section 521 applies to any farmers, fruit growers, or like associations organized and operated on a cooperative basis and only for marketing products or purchasing supplies and equipment.[156] The permitted purposes include (1) marketing products of members or other producers and turning back to them any net proceeds of sales on the basis of products furnished or (2) purchasing supplies and equipment for use by members or other persons and turning over to them such equipment at cost plus any necessary expenses.[157] To compute the allocable amount to patrons, the basis of products furnished for patrons may be determined by value or quantity of products furnished by patrons.[158]

b. Effect of Subchapter T on Section 521 Farmers' Cooperatives

Subchapter T modifies the taxation of Section 521 Farmers' Cooperatives in two ways. First, Subchapter T imposes regular corporate taxation on Section 521 farmers' cooperatives.[159] Second, it provides Section 521 farmers' cooperatives with special deductions, including special deductions that are unavailable to any other Subchapter T cooperative.[160] Nevertheless, for all other purposes under the Code, they are deemed exempt organizations.[161]

c. Flexibility of Section 521 Farmers' Cooperatives

The Code provides Section 521 farmers' cooperatives with some flexibility in determining their capital structure, dealing with nonmembers, and maintaining reserves. They may have capital stock as long as the cooperative satisfies two requirements. First, the dividend rate on such stock must not exceed the greater of (1) the legal rate permitted in the state of incorporation, or (2) eight percent annually, on the value given in exchange for such stock.[162] Second, substantially all such stock, except for certain nonvoting preferred stock,[163] must be owned by producers who market their products or purchase their supplies and equipment through the cooperative.[164]

Section 521 farmers' cooperatives may also market the products of, or purchase supplies for, nonmembers if the value of such marketing or purchases does not exceed the value of the products marketed for, or equipment purchased by, members.[165] In any case, the value of supplies and equipment purchased for persons who are neither members nor producers may not exceed fifteen percent of the value of all purchases made by the cooperative.[166] A member is anyone who is entitled to share in the profits and participate in the management of the cooperative.[167] In determining whether the cooperative complies with the limitations on transactions with nonmembers, the cooperative may disregard any business done with the U.S. government.[168]

While most cooperatives may maintain reserves to cover current costs, Section 521 farmers' cooperatives are expressly permitted to maintain reserves to the extent required by State law or for any necessary purpose.[169]

d. Nondiscrimination Rules

Section 521 farmers' cooperatives must operate on a cooperative basis. Inherent in cooperative operation is the obligation to return net earnings to patrons on the basis of patronage, regardless of whether a patron is a member of the cooperative.[170] The regulations expressly prohibit discrimination against nonmembers when distributing net earnings.[171] To explain, a Section 521 farmers' cooperative may not limit patronage dividends (or other distributions) to members, to the exclusion of nonmembers. Furthermore, to fulfill the requirement of proportionate and equitable distribution on the basis of patronage, the cooperative must keep permanent records of the business done with (or for) members and nonmembers.[172] Nonetheless, in certain situations, a Section 521 farmers' cooperative may treat patrons differently, depending upon whether patrons provide consent or agreement to include qualified notices[173] in gross income.[174]

3. Other Cooperative Organizations

The remaining nonexempt cooperatives receive no special treatment under Subchapter T. Like cooperatives subject to Subchapter T, however, these cooperatives are generally taxed as normal corporations and receive special deductions or other tax benefits under other sections of the Code.

a. Cooperative Housing Corporations

A cooperative housing corporation is a corporation organized to provide stockholders with the right to occupy a house or apartment building owned by the cooperative housing corporation.[175] The Code provides tax benefits at both the owner- and corporate-levels.[176] Although the corporation is generally taxed as any other corporation, additional tax benefits are provided to cooperative housing corporations and their tenant-stockholders.

Before discussing the tax benefits available to cooperative housing corporations and their tenant-shareholders, we must first establish a few definitions. A cooperative housing corporation is a corporation (1) that has only one class of stock outstanding, (2) each stockholder of which is entitled to occupy a house (including dwelling units and apartment buildings) owned by the corporation, solely as a result of ownership of such stock,[177] (3) no stockholder of which is entitled to receive any distribution except for an allocation of net earnings and profits, unless the corporation is liquidated, and (4) which, in years when the corporation claims the special deduction, satisfies one of three tests: a gross income test, an expenditure test, or a square footage test.[178] The gross income test requires the corporation to generate at least eighty percent of its gross income from tenant-stockholders.[179] The expenditure test requires that at least ninety percent of the corporation's expenditures are incurred for the acquisition, construction, management, maintenance, or care of the corporation's property.[180] The square footage test requires that at least eighty percent of the total square footage of the corporation's property is used or available for use by tenant-stockholders for residential or related purposes.[181]

A "tenant-stockholder" is defined as a person who is a stockholder in a cooperative housing corporation, but only if, in relation to such stock, the stockholder has "paid-up" an amount that bears a reasonable relationship to the value of the cooperative's equity in the houses and underlying land which the stockholder is entitled to occupy.[182]

Tax rules applicable to cooperative housing corporations provide tenant-stockholders with special deductions not generally available to other corporate stockholders.[183] A tenant-stockholder receives a deduction for the tenant-stockholder's proportionate share of the amount paid or accrued to the cooperative representing (1) real estate taxes, if deductible by the cooperative,[184] and (2) interest on debt incurred for the purpose of acquiring, constructing, altering, rehabilitating, or maintaining houses and purchasing land on which such houses are situated, but only to the extent such amount is deductable by the cooperative.[185] The purpose of these deductions is to treat tenant-stockholders similar to regular homeowners.[186]

Additionally, in some situations, tenant-stockholders may take depreciation deductions with respect to their stock, even though the cooperative housing corporation may also take depreciation deductions in the building.[187] Tenant-stockholders may take deductions for depreciation to the extent the tenant-shareholder's stock is treated as a proprietary lease or right of tenancy in property used in a trade or business or for the production of income (and thus subject to depreciation deductions).[188] A tenant-stockholder's depreciation deduction is limited to the amount of the stockholder's adjusted basis in the stock.[189]

Finally, cooperative housing corporations recognize no gain or loss on the distribution of a dwelling unit to a stockholder if the distribution is in exchange for the stockholder's stock, and the dwelling unit was used as the stockholder's principal residence.[190]

b. Cooperative Banks

A cooperative bank is an additional type of non-exempt cooperative that is not subject to the provisions of Subchapter T.[191] A "cooperative bank" is defined as an institution without capital stock that is organized and operated for mutual purposes and without profits, and (1) which is either an "insured institution" under the National Housing Act[192] or is subject to supervision and examination by a State or Federal authority, and (2) its business consists principally of acquiring the savings of the public and investing in loans, and at least sixty percent of its total assets at the close of the taxable year consists of certain specified assets.[193]

A cooperative bank receives special deductions for dividends paid to, or credited to the accounts of, depositors or holders of accounts as dividends or interest on their deposits or withdrawable accounts.[194] The deposits or withdrawable amounts must be withdrawable on demand, subject only to the organization's customary notice of intention to withdraw.[195] Certain cooperative banks may also qualify for a special deduction for additions to reserves for bad debt.[196]

E. Tax Exemption

The other system of taxation grants exemption from federal income taxation for certain cooperatives. In general, the most coveted tax status for business entities is tax exemption.[197] As one might expect, tax exemption is only granted when organizations meet certain restrictive criteria.

1. Section 501(c)(12) Cooperatives

Among the tax-exempt cooperatives are Section 501(c)(12) cooperatives. As a general rule, these tax-exempt cooperatives do not pay tax on their earnings. However, a few exceptions from this general rule might apply to impose taxation on some or all of the cooperative's income. For instance, unrelated business income of most tax-exempt organizations is taxable.[198] Additionally, as discussed in detail later, if a Section 501(c)(12) cooperative earns too much nonmember income, the cooperative is treated as a taxable cooperative.[199]

a. Applicability of § 501(c)(12)

The applicability of § 501(c)(12) rests on three tests[200] related to (1) the cooperative's activities and purpose, (2) its operation, and (3) the source and purpose of its income. If an organization fails any of these tests, the organization cannot qualify for § 501(c)(12) status.

i. Eligible Organizations and Purposes

The organizations which are eligible for exemption under § 501(c)(12) include

(1) benevolent life insurance associations of a purely local character,
(2) mutual ditch or irrigation companies,

(3) mutual or cooperative telephone companies, and
(4) like organizations.

Benevolent life insurance associations are the only organizations listed which are limited geographically, except for organizations claiming exemption based on their similarity to benevolent life insurance associations.[201] The geographically limiting phrase, "of a purely local character," means confined to a particular community, place, or district, but irrespective to political subdivisions.[202] However, confinement to the boundaries of a particular state does not necessarily satisfy the geographic limitation.[203]

Benevolent life insurance associations do not include organizations that issue policies for stipulated cash premiums.[204] They also exclude insurance associations that require advance deposits to cover the cost of insurance and maintain investments from which more than fifteen percent of its income is derived.[205]

The last option, "like organizations," actually expands exemption to many other types of organizations. However, a "like organization" must be similar in nature or purpose to the other organizations listed in § 501(c)(12)(A).[206] Like organizations include cooperatives which provide, among other things, rural electric[207] and cable television service[208] or light and water service,[209] or provide internet service.[210] The IRS has ruled that "like organizations" exclude organizations which solely finance consumer electrical appliances[211] or distribute and sale propane in tanks.[212] However, at one time the IRS was studying whether sales of electrical equipment would qualify as a like activity.[213]

ii. Operation on a Cooperative Basis

The second test relates to an organization's operation. To qualify as a Section 501(c)(12) cooperative, the organization must operate on a cooperative basis. The cooperative principles established in the *Puget Sound* case apply also to § 501(c)(12) cooperatives.[214] In addition, the IRS issued a questions and answer–style revenue ruling in 1972 that not only confirmed that the *Puget Sound* principles apply, but also clarified how those principles apply to Section 501(c)(12) cooperatives in particular.[215] Section 501(c)(12) cooperatives must (1) return earnings in proportion to patronage, (2) retain earning solely to meet the current losses and expenses and to maintain a reasonable reserve, (3) retain records regarding members' rights to retained earnings, (4) forbid forfeiture of members' rights in earnings upon termination, and (5) allocate any gain or loss from the sale of assets on dissolution to entities which were members while the cooperative owned the asset.[216]

Later, in 1977, the Ninth Circuit Court of Appeals held in *Peninsula Light Co., Inc. v. U.S.* that an organization that did not distribute earnings among its members on a patronage basis was still exempt under § 501(c)(12).[217] The organization's bylaws only provided for distribution of a gain on dissolution, and only among the members at the time of dissolution.[218] One year later, the IRS, in Revenue Ruling 78-238, announced it would not follow the holding of *Peninsula Light*. The IRS reasoned,

> The organization's method of operation was clearly in conflict with basic principles of mutual or cooperative operation. By failing to provide for computation of its members' interests on a patronage basis and by causing the forfeiture of former members' rights and interests upon termination of their membership, the organization failed to operate on a mutual or cooperative basis. It is the position of the Service that organizations that do not operate on a mutual or cooperative basis do not qualify for exemption under section 501(c)(12) of the Code.

It is now well settled that organizations seeking to qualify as exempt under § 501(c)(12) must operate on a cooperative basis.[219]

A common issue related to cooperative operation is whether a Section 501(c)(12) cooperative may retain reserves and still remain exempt. Revenue Ruling 72-36 indicates that a cooperative may retain excess reserves solely to meet current losses and expenses.[220] Current losses and expenses may include retiring indebtedness incurred in acquiring assets, expanding services and other necessary purposes, as long as the funds are not retained beyond the reasonable needs of the cooperative's business.[221]

iii. The Member Income Test

Section 501(c)(12) conditions exemption on satisfying a member income test. Under this test, the cooperative must collect at least eighty-five percent of its income from members, and solely for the purpose of meeting losses and expenses.[222] However, as discussed later, § 501(c)(12) excludes certain types of income from the test, and it reclassifies one type of non-member-sourced income as member-sourced income, regardless of the income's actual source.

Under the member income test, a cooperative must compute the ratio of income from member sources to income from all sources on an annual basis.[223] If that ratio is less than eighty-five percent, the organization must file a tax return as a taxable cooperative for that year.[224] To determine whether the cooperative satisfies this test, § 501(c)(12) excludes certain types of income for telephone cooperatives[225] and electric cooperatives,[226] and reclassifies one type of income generated by electric cooperatives as member income.[227]

b. Unrelated Business Income Tax

Section 511 imposes a tax on the unrelated business taxable income[228] of most exempt organizations.[229] The tax works the same as regular corporate tax, except it is only applicable to unrelated business income.[230] In general, unrelated business income means gross income generated from an unrelated trade or business that is regularly carried on by the organization.[231] "Unrelated trade or business" is defined as any trade or business that is not substantially related to the purpose or function constituting the basis for its exemption.[232] As a result, as long as income is substantially related to the § 501(c)(12) purpose (e.g., telephone, electric, water, or similar service), then the unrelated business income tax does not apply. Nevertheless, when such services are provided to nonmembers, the cooperative might run afoul of the member income test.[233]

2. Section 501(c)(14)—Credit Unions[234]

Section 501(c)(14) exempts credit unions without capital stock which are organized and operated for mutual purposes and without profit.[235] "A credit union is a democratically controlled cooperative nonprofit society organized for the purpose of encouraging thrift and self-reliance among its members by creating a source of credit at a fair and reasonable rate of interest in order to improve the economic and social conditions of its members."[236] In *Credit Union Ins. Corp. v. U.S.*, the Court held that a cooperative bank was not a credit union for purposes of IRC § 501(c)(14).[237]

3. Section 501(c)(16)—Cooperative Organizations to Finance Section 521 Farmers' Cooperative's Crop Operations

Section 501(c)(16) exempts corporations organized by Section 521 farmers' cooperatives or members of a Section 521 farmers' cooperative to finance crop operations of such members or other producers, if operated in conjunction with the Section 521 farmers' cooperative.[238] The requirements for exemption of such organizations are substantially similar to those for Section 521 farmers' cooperatives.[239] Just as with Section 521 farmers' cooperatives, Section 501(c)(16) cooperatives may issue capital stock[240] and may retain reasonable reserves.[241]

4. Section 501(e)—Cooperative Hospital Service Organizations

Section 501(e) clarifies and potentially expands the scope of exemption as a charitable organization[242] to organizations which are organized and operated exclusively for charitable purposes, as it applies to hospital service organizations.[243] The exemption applies only if the organization satisfies four tests related to (1) the operation of the organization, (2) its members, (3) earnings distribution, and (4) its capital stock.[244]

The operational test for exemption requires a Section 501(e) cooperative to perform one or more qualifying services on a centralized basis.[245] Such qualifying services, if performed directly by a tax-exempt hospital, would have constituted an activity in the performance or in furtherance of the hospital's exempt purpose.[246] Qualifying services include "data processing, purchasing (including the purchasing of insurance on a group basis), warehousing, billing and collection (including the purchase of patron accounts receivable on a recourse basis), food, clinical, industrial engineering, laboratory, printing, communications, record center, and personnel (including selection, testing, training, and education of personnel) services."[247]

In *Metropolitan Detroit Area Hospital Services, Inc. v. U.S.,*[248] the Court of Appeals for the Sixth Circuit held that a cooperative formed by six hospitals for the purpose of providing laundry services among the owner-hospitals was not exempt under § 501(e). The court reasoned that the list of exempt activities under § 501(e) was exclusively definitive, not a loosely inclusive description.[249] Nevertheless, such an organization could seek Subchapter T status if it otherwise qualified under Subchapter T.[250]

A Section 501(e) cooperative must have certain types of members. The members must either (1) qualify for exemption under § 501(c)(3), or (2) constitute a constituent part of a § 501(c)(3) organization, and if the § 501(e) cooperative were independent, it would qualify for § 501(c)(3) itself, or (3) be owned and operated by the United States, a state, the District of Columbia, or a possession of the United States.[251]

A Section 501(e) cooperative must, of course, be organized and operated on a cooperative basis.[252] In addition, it must allocate and pay all net earnings to its member-patrons on the basis of services provided to each member-patron within eight and one-half months following the taxable year.[253]

The last prong of the test for exemption only applies to Section 501(e) cooperatives which have capital stock.[254] For such cooperatives, the members must own all of any outstanding capital stock.[255]

5. Section 501(f)—Cooperative Service Organization of an Operating Educational Organization

Section 501(f) includes within the scope of charitable purposes the activities of cooperative service organizations of an operating educational organization.[256] An organization qualifies under § 501(f), and therefore may qualify for exemption under § 501(c)(3), if (1) such cooperative is organized and operated to collectively invest in stocks and securities, and to return any net earnings to such members, (2) such cooperative is organized and controlled by one or more members, and (3) the members of such cooperative meet certain requirements. The members must be educational organizations[257] or certain organizations which hold property for the benefit of such educational organizations,[258] and such members must be tax exempt.[259]

F. Conclusion

Recognizing cooperatives' unique nonprofit nature, Congress has historically provided cooperatives with tax benefits under the Code. However, to prevent abuse of these tax benefits, and presumably as a result of differing special interests in Congress, exceptions and special provisions permeate the Code. Whether a taxable cooperative seeks a special deduction under Subchapter T, or whether an exempt cooperative attempts to avoid unrelated business income tax, cooperatives must navigate federal tax law with care. Eventually, most cooperatives will find that no cooperative is completely impervious to the long arms of the Code.

Notes

1. Hereinafter IRS
2. Stated in IRC § 1381 for Subchapter T cooperatives.
3. Stated in IRC § 521 for farmers' cooperatives.
4. 44 T.C. 305 (1965).
5. *See* IRS Announcement 96-24 (discussing rules related to IRC § 501(c)(12) cooperatives).
6. For purposes of this chapter, we have assumed that a cooperative is a "business entity" pursuant to Reg. § 301.7701-2(a). An analysis of this issue is beyond the scope of this chapter.
7. As used herein, the term "taxable entity" should be distinguished from the term "business entity," as used in the "Check-The-Box" Regulations, discussed in detail below. Under these Regulations, "business entity" includes "any entity recognized for federal tax purposes (including an entity with a single owner that may be disregarded as an entity separate from its owner . . .)." Reg. § 301.7701-2(a). Thus, business entities include disregarded entities. As used in this chapter, the term "taxable entity" does not include disregarded entities.
8. *See e.g.,* Treas. Reg. § 301.7701-2(b)(1); Priv. Ltr. Rul. 200139020 (Jun. 29, 2001).
9. As a practical matter, virtually every cooperative is a taxable entity due to its number of owners. This rule is discussed in more detail in the following.
10. Check-the-box regulations earned their name as a result of the ease with which eligible entities can choose their form of tax classification. Treas. Reg. §§ 301.7701-1 to 301.7701-3.
11. Treas. Reg. § 301.7701-2(a).
12. *Id.*
13. *Id.*
14. Treas. Reg. § 301.7701-3(a).
15. Treas. Reg. § 301.7701-3(a).
16. Treas. Reg. § 301.7701-2(a). Treas. Reg. § 301.7701-1 provides guidance on whether an entity or undertaking is recognized as separate from its owner for federal tax purposes.
17. Treas. Reg. § 301.7701-2(b).
18. Even if an entity is not a "taxable entity," it still may have obligations to file certain tax returns or informational returns, and may even be subject to other types of taxation (e.g., excise and employment taxes). The most common example is a partnership, which must file Form 1065 ("U.S. Return of Partnership Income").
19. *See* MEADE EMORY & WILLIAM P. STRENG, FEDERAL INCOME TAXATION OF CORPORATIONS & SHAREHOLDERS: FORMS § 1.06(5) (2007).

20. *See* Subchapter T, IRC §§ 1381–1388. As discussed later, cooperatives organized under a corporation statute could not elect partnership treatment because such entities are generally "per se corporations." In contrast, most limited liability companies with multiple-owners could elect corporate or partnership treatment.

21. *See* IRC § 1385.

22. *See* EMORY, *supra* note 18 at § 1.06(5).

23. Priv. Ltr. Rul. 200139020 (Sept. 28, 2001).

24. As explained, the term "deduction," as used by the Code, actually has two different applications. Depending on the type of patronage dividend, Subchapter T permits (1) subtractions from income to compute gross income and (2) subtractions from gross income to compute taxable income. As used herein, depending on the context, "deduction" could indicate to either meaning.

25. For purposes of this discussion, "corporate" and "corporation" refer to corporations subject to Subchapter C and not to corporations subject to Subchapter S.

26. *See* IRC § 11 for the general rule of taxation of corporate income. As for the alternative taxation of net capital gains of corporations, *see* IRC § 1201.

27. See the discussion below regarding the "exempt" status of Section 521 farmers' cooperatives.

28. *See* IRC § 1381.

29. The Code refers to Section 521 farmers' cooperatives as tax exempt. For purposes of this chapter, Section 521 farmers' cooperatives are considered along with other Subchapter T (taxable) cooperatives. *See* S. Rep. No. 1881, 87th Cong, 2d Sess. 311 (1962).

30. IRC § 801, *et seq.*

31. "Special Deduction" is not the term used by the Code. It is used herein, for the sake of succinctness, to refer to all deductions exclusively permitted by Subchapter T.

32. IRC § 1382(b).

33. *E.g.*, charitable contribution deductions under IRC § 170 and net operating loss deductions under IRC § 172.

34. IRC § 1382(c).

35. *See* IRC § 1388(j)(4).

36. IRC § 1388(j)(1). IRC § 521(b)(6) expressly applies this rule to Section 521 farmers' cooperatives.

37. IRC § 1388(j)(1).

38. IRC § 1388(j)(3). For netting rules in the year following a corporate acquisition under IRC § 381, *see* IRC § 1388(j)(2).

39. IRC § 1388(a); Treas. Reg. 1.1388-1(a)(1).

40. Hereinafter, such income shall be referred to as "patronage-sourced income" or "patronage-sourced earnings." Net earnings from patronage-sourced income shall be referred to as "patronage-sourced net income" or "patronage-sourced net earnings."

41. *See* Treas. Reg. § 1.1388-1(a).

42. The computation of patronage dividends is not necessarily performed in the chronological order presented herein.

43. Treas. Reg. § 1.1388-1(a)(1).

44. *Id.*

45. IRC § 1388(a)(last paragraph).

46. Treas. Reg. § 1.1388-1(a)(1).
47. *See* Reg. § Treas. Reg. § 1.1388-1(a)(1).
48. H.R. Rep. No. 108-548(I), at 148 (2004).
49. American Jobs Creation Act of 2004, Pub. L. No. 108-357, § 312, 118 Stat. 1418, 1467 (2004).
50. The 2004 amendment does not put Subchapter T cooperatives on equal footing with IRC § 521 farmers' cooperatives, which are permitted a special dividend for certain dividends on capital stock. Instead, it simply allows cooperatives to issue capital stock dividends without a corresponding reduction in their patronage earnings. A nonagricultural Subchapter T cooperatives must still distribute the earnings in a manner that qualifies for a special deduction (e.g., as a patronage dividend in cash or qualified notice of written allocation). Further, the 2004 amendment only applies to capital stock dividends to the extent that the cooperative is bound to distribute such dividends in addition to amounts otherwise due to patrons out of patronage net earnings. *See id.*; IRC § 1388(a)(1) (last paragraph).
51. For purposes of Subchapter T and § 521, marketing the products of members or other producers includes the feeding of such products to cattle, hogs, fish, chickens, or other animals and the sale of the resulting animals or animal products. IRC § 1388(k). IRC § 521(b)(7) references this rule as it applies to Section 521 farmers' cooperatives.
52. *See e.g.*, Rev. Rul. 69-576, 1969-2 C.B. 166 (1969); Treas. Reg. § 1.1382-3(c)(2); 9 MERTENS LAW OF FED. INCOME TAX'N § 34A:14 (2007).
53. Rev. Rul. 69-576.
54. IRC § 1388(a)(3).
55. IRC § 1388(a)(2).
56. Treas. Reg. § 1.1388-1(a)(1)(last paragraph).
57. Treas. Reg. § 1.1388-1(a)(1)(ii).
58. IRC § 1388(a).
59. Treas. Reg. § 1.1388-1(a)(2)(ii).
60. Treas. Reg. § 1.1388-1(a)(2)(iii).
61. Treas. Reg. § 1.1388-1(a)(2)(iv).
62. IRC § 1388(b).
63. Treas. Reg. § 1.1388-1(b).
64. IRC § 1388(b).
65. IRC § 1382(b)(1).
66. IRC § 1382(b)(2).
67. IRC § 1388(c)(1)(A). The cooperative must give the recipient a written notice of the right of redemption at the time of receipt. Notice must be given to each and every patron who receives a qualified written notice of allocation. Therefore, posting a notice in the local newspaper is insufficient. Treas. Reg. § 1.1388-1(c)(2).
68. IRC § 1388(c)(1)(B).
69. IRC § 1388(c)(1)(last sentence). "Qualified Check" is defined in IRC § 1388(c)(4).
70. Treas. Reg. § 1.1388-1(c)(3).
71. IRC § 1388(d).
72. IRC § 1388(f).
73. IRC § 1388(g).
74. IRC § 1388(h)(1). See IRC § 1385(a) regarding the recognition of taxable income by patrons.

75. IRC § 1388(h)(2).
76. IRC § 1388(i).
77. IRC § 1382(b)(1).
78. "Payment Period" is an important term used in Subchapter T for accounting purposes. See the section below entitled "Timing Rules for Special Deductions."
79. IRC § 1382(b)(1).
80. IRC § 1382(b)(2); Treas. Reg. § 1.1382-2(c).
81. IRC § 1382(b)(2).
82. This might occur because the payment period for a taxable year actually extends beyond the end of the taxable year and, therefore, into the following taxable year.
83. Treas. Reg. § 1.1382-2(c).
84. *Id.*
85. *Id.*
86. *Id.*
87. IRC § 1388(f).
88. For example, a farmer may transfer produce to the cooperative to sell on the farmer's behalf.
89. IRC § 1382(b)(3).
90. IRC § 1382(b)(4).
91. *Id.*
92. Treas. Reg. § 1.1382-3(a)(1).
93. IRC § 1382(c)(1).
94. Treas. Reg. § 1.1382-3(b).
95. *Id.*
96. *Id.*
97. *Id.*
98. IRC § 1382(c)(2)(A).
99. *Id.*
100. Treas. Reg. § 1.1382-3(c)(2).
101. Treas. Reg. § 1.1382-3(c)(3).
102. *See e.g.,* Treas. Reg. § 1.1382-3(c)(3).
103. Treas. Reg. § 1.1382-3(c)(1).
104. *Id.*
105. *Id.*
106. IRC § 1382(c)(2)(B).
107. *Id.*
108. Treas. Reg. § 1.1382-3(d).
109. *Id.; c.f.* Treas. Reg. § 1.1382-2(b).
110. IRC § 1382(d); Treas. Reg. § 1.1382-4.
111. IRC § 1382(d).
112. IRC § 1388(c)(4).
113. IRC § 1382(e); Treas. Reg. § 1.1382-5. See also § 1382(g) for the "completed crop pool method of accounting," available to certain pooling arrangements entered prior to March 1, 1978.
114. Treas. Reg. § 1.1382-5.
115. IRC § 1382(e).
116. IRC § 1382(f); Treas. Reg. § 1.1382-6.
117. Rev. Rul. 70-249, 1970-1 C.B. 181 (1970).

118. IRC § 1383(a).
119. Treas. Reg. 1.1383-1(d).
120. Under § 1382(b)(2) or § 1382(c)(2)(B).
121. Under § 1382(b)(4).
122. *See* IRC § 1383(a).
123. *See* IRC §§ 1382(b)(1), 1382(b)(3), & 1382(c)(2)(A).
124. As explained later, the decrease in tax usually gives rise to a credit or refund. *See* IRC § 1383(b)(1); Treas. Reg. § 1.1383-1(c).
125. IRC § 1383(a).
126. Treas. Reg. § 1.1383-1(b)(1).
127. Treas. Reg. § 1.1383-1(b)(3). Items dependent on gross income might include net operating losses, foreign tax credits, and dividends-received deductions. *Id.*
128. IRC § 1383(b)(1); Treas. Reg. § 1.1383-1(c). See the rules regarding overpayment of taxes at IRC § 6151.
129. IRC § 1383(b)(3); Treas. Reg. § 1.1383-1(a)(2).
130. Treas. Reg. § 1.1383-1(a)(3).
131. IRC § 1383(b)(3). However, Treas. Reg. § 1.1383-1(a)(2) states the deduction may be used in computing the current year's earnings and profits.
132. *See* IRC § 61.
133. IRC § 61(a). This section begins with the following qualifier: "Except as otherwise provided in this subtitle . . .," referring to Subtitle A ("Income Taxes") of Title 26 of the U.S. Code. Being within Subtitle A, IRC § 1385 modifies the general rule of IRC § 61(a) in the circumstances noted therein.
134. Treas. Reg. § 1.61-5(h).
135. IRC § 1385(a); Treas. Reg. § 1.1385-1(a). Inclusion does not depend on when the cooperative takes a corresponding deduction. The deduction may occur before or after the patron recognizes income.
136. *Id.*
137. As indicated, "nonqualified notice" includes nonqualified written notices of allocation and nonqualified per-unit retain certificates.
138. IRC § 1385(c)(2)(C).
139. *Id.*
140. Treas. Reg. § 1.1385-1(b)(1). Such income is deemed income from the sale of property other than a capital asset. *Id.*
141. *Id.*
142. IRC § 1385(c)(2)(A).
143. *Id.*
144. The regulations provide "Special Rules" governing exclusions from gross income under Subchapter T. *See* Treas. Reg. § 1.1385-1(c)(2).
145. *See* the examples under Treas. Reg. § 1.1385-1(c)(3).
146. IRC § 1385(b).
147. "Capital Asset" is defined in IRC § 1221.
148. Treas. Reg. § 1.1385-1(c); 9 Mertens Law of Fed. Income Tax'n § 34A:45 (2007). "Depreciable property" is property subject to depreciation under § 167.
149. Treas. Reg. § 1.1385-1(c)(3).
150. *See* IRC § 1012.
151. *See e.g.*, Internal Revenue Manual § 4.44.1.1.2 (Jan. 1, 2002).

116   Taxation of Cooperatives

152. IRC § 1381(b); Treas. Reg. § 1.522-2(a).
153. IRC § 521(a).
154. It would appear that the practical effect of the special deductions that apply only to farmers' cooperatives would limit taxation to very little, if any, income of farmers' cooperatives.
155. Whether a cooperative is labeled tax exempt may be of lesser importance than the type of earnings generated by the cooperative. Even tax-exempt cooperatives are subject to tax on certain transactions. *See e.g.*, IRC § 511 (relating to unrelated business income tax) and IRC § 501(c)(12) (imposing a limitation on income from nonmembers).
156. The regulations extend "like associations" to livestock growers and dairymen. Treas. Reg. § 1.521-1(a)(1).
157. IRC § 521(b)(1).
158. *Id.*
159. IRC § 1381(b).
160. Treas. Reg. § 1.1381-2(a)(1).
161. *Id.*
162. IRC § 521(b)(2).
163. Nonvoting preferred stock is not considered for this purpose if the owners of such stock are not entitled to participate in the profits of the cooperative, directly or indirectly and on dissolution or otherwise, beyond any fixed dividends. *Id.*
164. IRC § 521(b)(2).
165. IRC § 521(b)(4).
166. *Id.*
167. Treas. Reg. § 1.521-1(a)(3).
168. IRC § 521(b)(5).
169. IRC § 521(b)(3).
170. *See* Puget Sound, *supra* note 4.
171. Treas. Reg. § 1.521-1(a)(1).
172. *Id.* In lieu of distributing patronage dividends, a Section 521 farmers' cooperative may give nonmembers a credit toward the purchase of stock or membership in the cooperative. *Id.*
173. As noted, "qualified notices" include qualified notices of written allocation and qualified per-unit retain certificates.
174. Treas. Reg. § 1.521-1(f).
175. IRC § 216(b)(1).
176. 34 Am. Jur. Fed. Tax'n 2d § 20202 (2007).
177. As used herein, "house" includes a dwelling unit and an apartment building.
178. IRC § 216(b)(1).
179. *Id.*
180. *Id.*
181. *Id.*
182. IRC § 216(b)(2).
183. IRC § 216(a).
184. *See* IRC § 164.
185. *See* IRC § 163.
186. Eckstein v. U.S., 452 F.2d 1036, 1047-48, 196 Ct.Cl. 644, 644 (1971).
187. IRC § 216(c) (referencing § 167(a)).
188. IRC § 216(c).

Notes 117

189. IRC § 216(c)(2)(A). Any disallowed depreciation may, if permitted by § 216(c)(2)(A), be applied in future tax years. IRC § 216(c)(2)(B).

190. IRC § 216(e). See IRC § 121 to determine whether the house will be deemed used by the taxpayer as his or her principal residence.

191. Subchapter H, Part II of the Code (IRC §§ 591–597) applies to cooperative banks, among other similar organizations. Subchapter T expressly excludes from its scope those organizations governed by Part II of Subchapter H. IRC § 1381(a)(2)(B)(i); Treas. Reg. § 1.1381-1(b)(2). Note also that credits unions are exempt under IRC § 501(c)(14), which is discussed below.

192. See § 401(a) of National Housing Act.

193. IRC § 7701(a)(32). This section imports some of the requirements of § 7701(a)(19), relating to domestic building and loan associations. 34 AM. JUR. FED. TAX'N § 20476 (2007). The specified assets are listed in IRC § 7701(a)(19).

194. IRC § 591(a).

195. Id.

196. IRC § 593(a). The cooperative bank must meet the "sixty percent asset test" of § 7701(a)(19). This special deduction is in lieu of the deduction allowed under § 166(a).

197. See e.g., IRC § 501(a), which exempts those organizations listed in IRC § 501(c).

198. See IRC § 511

199. IRS Announcement 96-24.

200. IRS Announcement 96-24; MICHAEL SETO & CHERYL CHASIN, GENERAL SURVEY OF IRC 501(C)(12) COOPERATIVES AND EXAMINATION OF CURRENT ISSUES, IRS Exempt Organization Continuing Professional Education (CPE) Technical Instruction Program (2002).

201. Treas. Reg. § 1.501(c)(12)-1(b).

202. Id.

203. Id.

204. Treas. Reg. § 1.501(c)(12)-1(a).

205. Id. This rule does not apply to advance assessments for the sole purpose of meeting future losses and expenses.

206. Rev. Rul. 65-201, 1965-2 C.B. 170 (1965); Gen. Couns. Mem. 38,511 (Sept. 26, 1980).

207. See IRC § 501(c)(12)(C).

208. IRS Announcement 96-24.

209. Rev. Rul. 67-265, 1967-2 C.B. 205 (1967).

210. Priv. Ltr. Rul. 200504035 (2005).

211. Consumers Credit Rural Elec. Co-op. Corp. v. C.I.R., 37 T.C. 136, 142-43 (1961).

212. Rev. Rul. 2002-54, 2002-2 C.B. 527 (2002).

213. SETO, *supra* note 196 at p. 187.

214. Announcement 96-24.

215. Rev. Rul. 72-36, 1972-1 C.B. 151 (1972).

216. Id.

217. Peninsula Light Co., Inc. v. U.S., 552 F.2d 878 (9th Cir. 1977).

218. Id.

219. Announcement 96-24; SETO, *supra* note 196 at p. 178.

220. Rev. Rul. 72-36.

221. *Id.*

222. IRC § 501(c)(12)(A).

223. *See e.g.*, Treas. Reg. § 1.501(c)(12)-1(c) (providing an example of the ratio for telephone cooperatives, with exclusions of certain types of income).

224. IRS Announcement 96-24.

225. For example, under IRC § 501(c)(12)(B), telephone cooperatives may exclude from the test any income from (1) nonmember telephone companies for the performance of communication services which involve members of the cooperative, (2) qualified pole rentals, (3) member directory listings, and (4) the prepayment of certain loans.

226. Electric cooperatives may exclude (1) qualified pole rentals, (2) sales of certain "electric energy transmission services" or ancillary services, (3) certain sales of certain "electric energy distribution services," (4) income from nuclear decommissioning transactions, and (5) income from any "asset exchange or conversion transaction." IRC § 501(c)(12)(C). Further, the IRS has broadly stated in Publication 557 that electric cooperatives may exclude the sale of excess fuel at cost in the year of purchase. *See* IRS Publication 557 (2005); *c.f.* Rev. Rul. 80-86, 1980- C.B. 118 (Mar. 31, 1980).

227. Electric cooperatives may reclassify certain income from nonmember sources as income from member sources collected for the sole purpose of meeting losses and expenses. Income from load loss transactions are treated as member income, regardless of whether they are actually received from a member. IRC § 501(c)(12)(H). For a definition of "Load Loss Transaction," *see* § 501(c)(12)(H). This rule also applies to taxable electric cooperatives. IRC § 501(c)(12)(H)(i). Furthermore, income from load loss transactions is exempt from the unrelated business income tax of § 511. IRC § 501(c)(12)(H)(ix).

228. "Unrelated Business Taxable Income" is defined in IRC § 512, and "Unrelated Business Income" in IRC § 513.

229. IRC § 511(a).

230. *Id.*

231. IRC § 512(a)(1).

232. IRC § 513(a).

233. As noted, income from load loss transactions is not only treated as member-sourced (irrespective of the actual source), it is entirely exempt from the § 511 unrelated business income tax. IRC § 512(b)(18).

234. For a discussion on cooperative banks, see the section entitled "Cooperative Banks."

235. IRC § 501(c)(14)(A).

236. Rev. Rul. 85-175, 1983-2 C.B. 109 (1983) (obsoleted on other grounds by Treas. Decision 8734, 62 F.R. 53387-1 (Oct. 14, 1997)); BITTKER & LOKKEN: FEDERAL TAXATION OF INCOME, ESTATES, AND GIFTS § 102.9 (2007).

237. *See* Credit Union Ins. Corp. v. U.S., 86 F.3d 1326, 1329 (4th Cir. 1996) (corporation did not qualify for exemption under IRC § 501(c)(14)(B) as providing deposit insurance to "cooperative banks" where corporation instead provided deposit insurance to "credit unions").

238. IRC § 501(c)(16).

239. Treas. Reg. § 1.501(c)(16)-1.

240. IRC § 501(c)(16). Such organizations may only have capital stock only if (1) the dividend rate does not exceed the greater of the legal rate of interest in the

state of incorporation or eight percent annually, both computed based upon the value given for such stock, and (2) substantially all of such stock (except certain nonvoting preferred stock) is owned by the cooperative or its members. *Id.*

241. *Id.*
242. *See* IRC § 501(c)(3).
243. IRC § 501(e).
244. 9 MERTENS LAW OF FED. INCOME TAX'N § 34:46 (2007).
245. IRC § 501(e)(1)(A).
246. *Id.*
247. *Id.*
248. 634 F.2d 330, 334 (6th Cir. 1980).
249. *See also* HCSC-Laundry v. U.S., 450 U.S. 1 (1981).
250. Rev. Rul. 69-633, 1969-2 C.B. 121 (1969).
251. IRC § 501(e)(1)(B). As used herein, any reference to a governmental entity includes any agency or instrumentality of such entity.
252. IRC § 501(e)(2).
253. *Id.* Compare this requirement with the "payment period" under Subchapter T at IRC § 1382(d); Treas. Reg. § 1.1382-4.
254. IRC § 501(e)(3).
255. *Id.*
256. IRC § 501(f).
257. *See* the requirements in IRC § 170(b)(1)(A)(ii).
258. *See* the requirements in IRC § 170(b)(1)(A)(iv).
259. IRC § 501(f)(3).

Table of Cases

Atchison County Farmers Union Coop. Ass'n v. Turnbull,
736 P.2d 917 (Kan. 1987) 86

Bontrager v. La Plata Elec. Ass'n Inc., 68 P.3d 555
(Colo. App. 2003) 52

Burley Tobacco Soc'y v. Gillaspy, 100 N.E. 89
(Ind. App. 1912) 23

Burns v. Wray Farmers' Grain Co., 176 P. 487 (Colo. 1918) 23

Claassen v. Farmers Grain Co-op., 490 P.2d 376 (Kan. 1971) 85

Commonwealth v. Hodges, 125 S.W. 689 (Ky. App. 1910) 23

Consumers Credit Rural Elec. Co-op. Corp. v. C.I.R.,
37 T.C. 136, 142-43 (1961) 117

Credit Union Ins. Corp. v. U.S., 86 F.3d 1326, 1329
(4th Cir. 1996) 118

Eckstein v. U.S., 452 F.2d 1036, 1047-48, 196 Ct.Cl. 644,
644 (1971) 116

Frost v. Corp. Comm'n of State of Okla., 278 U.S. 515,
546 (1929) 22

Ga. Turkey Farms, Inc. v. Hardigree, 369 S.E.2d 803
(Ga. App. 1988) 85

Great Rivers Co-op. of Southeastern Iowa v. Farmland
Indus., Inc., 198 F.3d 685 (8th Cir. 1999) 85

HCSC-Laundry v. U.S., 450 U.S. 1 (1981) 118

Howard v. Eatonton Coop. Feed Co., 177 S.E.2d 658
(Ga. 1970) 86

In re FCX, Inc., 853 F.2d 1149 (4th Cir. 1988) 86

In re Greensboro Lumber Co., 157 B.R. 921
(Bankr. M.D. Ga. 1993) 86

Kavanaugh v. Commonwealth Trust Co., 119 N.E. 237,
238 (N.Y. 1918) 70

Lake Region Packing Ass'n, Inc. v. Furze, 327 So.2d 212
(Fla. 1976) 85

Lambert v. Fisherman's Dock Coop., Inc., 280 A.2d 193,
197 (N.J. Super. Ct. App. Div. 1971) 85

Lewis v. Jackson Energy Co-op Corp., 189 S.W.2d 87
(Ky. 2005) 52

Litwin v. Allen, 25 N.Y.S.2d 667, 677 (N.Y. Sup. Ct. 1940) 18

Md. & Va. Milk Producers Ass'n v. United States,
362 U.S. 458, 468 (1960) 23

Peninsula Light Co., Inc. v. U.S., 552 F.2d 878
(9th Cir. 1977) 118

Reeves v. Decorah Farmers' Co-operative Soc'y,
140 N.W. 844 (Iowa 1913) 23

Tobacco Growers Co-operative Ass'n v. Jones,
117 S.E. 174, 179 (N.C. 1923) 23

Weber v. Interbel Tel. Co-op, Inc., 80 P.3d 88
(Mont. 2003) 52

Index

Ace Hardware, 4, 48
America, early cooperatives, 12–13
American Farm Bureau Federation, 18
Annan, Kofi, on cooperatives, 5

Base capital plan, 85
Blue Diamond Growers, 17, 50–51
Board of directors, 30–31, 56–60
    distinctive characteristics, 58–59
    duties, 62–68
    judging performance of, 59
    liability and training, 59–60
    objective viewpoint as a challenge, 59
    selection and compensation, 57–58
    training programs for, 60
Business purpose, 29–31
    categories of cooperatives, 44–49
Bylaws, preparation for a cooperative, 38–39

Capital, 74–79. *See also* specific type
Capitalization, 71–86
Capper-Volstead Act, 16–17
Centralized cooperatives, 50–51
Civil War, cooperative development after, 13–20
Clayton Act, 16–17
CoBank, 78
Common stock, 72–73
Conceptual relationships, cooperative and its members, 68–69

Consumer cooperatives, 4, 45
Control and decision-making, 35–36
Cooperative banks, 105–106
Cooperative housing corporations, 104–105
Cooperative Marketing Act of 1926, 10, 17
Cooperatives
    basic description, 1–3
    capitalization and finance, 71–86
    categories, 41–52
    classification by business purpose, 42–49
    classification by structure, 49–52
    comparison to other entities, 2
    comparison with other business entities, 26–32
    conceptual relationship with members, 68–69
    corporate taxation with special benefits, 90–106
    definitions, 7–8
    development of, 2
    duties of officers and directors, 62–68
    early American, 12–13
    England, 10–12
    for Federal Tax purposes, 87–88
    formation of, 36–40
    how is it taxed?, 90
    importance in U.S. and world economies, 4–5
    intangible differences, 3

Index

Cooperatives, *continued*
  new types, 20–22
  officers and management, 61–62
  one product or service, 3
  operation and governance, 53–70
  origins, 10–22
  principles, 8–10
  state statutes, 37
  tax exemption, 106–110
  taxation, 87–119
  when to use, 32–36
Corporate taxation, special benefits to cooperatives, 90–106
Credit Union National Association, training programs for directors, 60
Credit Unions, as cooperatives, 4, 18

Debt capital, 77–79
Directors. *See* Board of directors
Distribution of income, 29–31
Duty of care, 62–63
Duty of loyalty, 63–65
Duty of obedience, 65

Educational programs, 9–10
England, emergence of cooperatives, 10–12
Equity capital, 75–77
  allocated and unallocated, 76–77
  in new generation cooperatives, 77
Equity redemption plans, 82–85

Farm bureaus, 18
Farm Credit System, 78
Farm Loan Act of 1916, 16–17
Farm Security Administration (FSA), 18–19
Federal Credit Union Act, 1934, 18
Federal Land Bank, 16–17
Federal tax, definition of a cooperative, 87–88
Federated Cooperatives, 51
Fiduciary duty, officers and directors, 62–68
Financing techniques, 27–29, 71–86
Franklin, Benjamin, first successful cooperative in America, 12

Georgia Electric Membership Corporation Act, 57

Hybrid or mixed cooperatives, 501–52

Indemnity, protection, 67–68
Industrial Revolution, cooperatives and, 10–11
Insurance, officers and directors, 67–68
Internal Revenue Code (IRS), cooperatives, 88
International Co-operative Alliance, 5
  definition, 7–8
Internet Corporation of Assigned Names and Numbers (ICANN), 5

Land O'Lakes, 4, 47, 51
Liability
  minimizing for officers and management, 65–67
  protection, 67–68
Limited liability company (LLC), 20–22
Lines of business, restrictions, 34, 42–44

Manager/CEO, cooperative structure, 61
Marketing cooperatives, 4
Massachusetts Mutual Life Company, 13
Member income test, 108
Members, 53–56. *See also* Owners
  conceptual relationship with cooperative, 68–69
  governance power, 55–56
  relation to the cooperative, 54–55
Metropolitan Detroit Area Hospital Services, Inc. v. U.S., 110
Modern cooperative, emergence, 10–12
Mondragon Cooperative Corporation, 49
Mutual of Omaha, 4

Index

National Association of Housing Cooperatives, 10
National Conference of Commissioners on Uniform State Laws (NCCUSL), 22
National Cooperative Bank, 46
National Cooperative Business Association, 10
National Farmers Union, 18
National Grange, 13–14
National Rural Electric Cooperative Association, training programs for directors, 60
National Rural Utilities Cooperative Finance Corporation (CFC), 78
Nationwide Mutual Insurance Company, 4
Net margins, 77–82
New Deal, 19
New England Protective Union, 12
Nonprofit nature, cooperative challenge, 59
Nonqualified per-unit retain certificates, 97
Nonqualified written notices of allocation, redemption, 96
Nonstock cooperative, 37
  comparison of stock cooperative, 37
Northwestern Mutual Life Insurance Company, 13

Ocean Spray, 17, 47
Officers and management, 61–62
  duties, 62–68
Oglethorpe Power Corporation, 51
One-member/one-vote principle, 31, 56
Operation and governance, 53–70
Outside investment, restrictions, 35
Owner/customers, 2
Owners as customers, cooperative challenge, 58–59
Ownership and control, cooperative entities, 29–31
Oxford Provident Building Association of Philadelphia, 13

Patron, 79
Patronage dividends, 93–94
Patronage earnings and losses, 92
Patronage refunds, 77–82
Payment of dividends, restrictions, 35
Per-unit retain allocation and certificate, 95–97
Philadelphia Contributorship for the Insurance of Homes from Loss of Fire, 12
Preferred stock, 73–74
Producer/marketing cooperatives, 46–48
Puget Consumers Co-op, 45
Puget Sound Plywood, Inc. v. C. I. R., 88
Purchasing cooperatives, 48

Quayside Art Gallery, 47–48

Return on investment, 27–29
Revolving fund plan, 84
Rochdale Society of Equitable Pioneers, England, 8–9, 11–12
Roosevelt, Franklin, boost to cooperatives, 18–19
Rural Electrification Act (REA), 18–19
Rural Utilities Service, 19

Sarbanes-Oxley Act of 2002, 60
Savings and loan association, early American cooperatives, 13
Section 521 Farmers' Cooperatives
  applicability, 103
  dividends on capital stock, 97
  effect of Subchapter T, 103
  flexibility, 103–104
  non-patronage earnings and U.S. government sources, 97–98
  non-patronage sources and U.S. government sources, 98–99
  nondiscrimination rules, 104
  tax exemption, 109
Section 501(c)(16)—cooperative organizations to finance Section 521 operations, 109

Index

Section 501(c)(12) companies, 106–109
Section 501(c)(14) credit unions, 109
Section 502(e)—cooperative hospital service organizations, 109–110
Section 502(e)—cooperative service organization of an operating educational organization, 110
Service cooperatives, 45–46
Shareholders, comparison to members, 54–55
Sherman Antitrust Act, 1890, 15–16
Southeastern Data Cooperative, 46
Southern California Fruit Exchange, 17
St. Mary's Bank Credit Union of Manchester, New Hampshire, 18
State Farm Insurance, 4
State statutes, relating to cooperatives, 37
Stock cooperative, 37
　comparison of nonstock cooperative, 71–74
Subchapter T cooperatives
　applicability, 91
　definitions applicable, 92–95
　special deductions, 91–92
　special tax computation, 100–101
　taxation of patrons, 101–102
　types of special deductions, 96–99
Sun-Maid, 47
Sunkist Growers, 4, 47
Sunsweet, 47

Taxable entity, cooperative as, 88–90
Taxation, 31–32, 87–119
Tennessee Valley Authority (TVA), 83
Texas Agricultural Cooperative Council, training programs for directors, 60
Timing rules, 99–100
Traditional cooperative, 8
Tree Top, 47

U.S. Department of Agriculture (USDA)
　cooperative education, 10
　definition, 8
　educational and financial assistance, 48
　Rural Utilities Service, 78, 83
U.S. Federation of Worker Cooperatives, 49
Unified Foodservice Purchasing Co-op, 48
Uniform Limited Cooperative Association Act (LCAA), 22
United Nations, 5
United States economy, cooperatives in, 4–5
Unrelated business income tax, 108–109

Welch's, 47
Worker cooperatives, 48–49
World economy, cooperatives in, 4–5
Written notice of allocation, 94–95

About the Authors

Charles T. Autry is a partner in the law firm of Autry, Horton, & Cole, LLP, with offices in Atlanta, Georgia, and Tucker, Georgia. For the past thirty years, his legal career has focused on the representation of cooperatives with an emphasis on electric and natural gas cooperatives. He has extensive experience in the negotiation and drafting of complex power supply, natural gas, and construction contracts for cooperatives and in corporate and financial matters involving cooperative electric and gas utilities. In addition, he serves as counsel to several cooperative boards of directors.

Mr. Autry received his B.A. from the University of Georgia, his J.D. from the University of Alabama School of Law, his M.B.A. from Georgia State University, and his Master of Laws in Taxation from the Emory University School of Law. After receiving his J.D., he served in the U.S. Marine Corps as a Captain in the Judge Advocate Division.

Mr. Autry is a member of the Electric Cooperative Bar Association, the State Bar of Georgia, and the American Bar Association. He is past chairman of the Georgia Electric Membership Corporation Counsel Association. He has been a frequent speaker on topics involving rural electric cooperatives. He is admitted to practice in Georgia and the District of Columbia.

Roland F. Hall is a partner in the law firm of Autry, Horton, & Cole, LLP. His practice includes representing electric cooperatives and related entities in corporate; finance and regulatory matters; negotiating and drafting contracts, including construction contracts; and handling complex business transactions and commercial litigation.

Mr. Hall received his B.A. magna cum laude in English and mathematics from Mercer University, and his J.D. magna cum laude from the Mercer University Walter F. George School of Law. He was Senior Managing Editor of the Mercer Law Review. He served as Judicial Clerk to U.S. District Judge Roger Vinson in Pensacola, Florida, and to U.S. District Judge Robert Hinkle in Tallahassee, Florida.

Mr. Hall is a member of the State Bar of Georgia, Florida Bar, American Bar Association, and Electric Cooperative Bar Association. He is admitted to practice law in Georgia and Florida.